Spider Woman's Children

NAVAJO WEAVERS TODAY

Lynda Teller Pete and Barbara Teller Ornelas
Photography by Joe Coca

Editor/Publisher: Linda Ligon
Associate Editor/Publisher: Karen Brock
Photographer: Joe Coca
Designer: Michael Angelo Signorella

Text ©2018 Barbara Teller Ornelas and Lynda Teller Pete
Photography: Joe Coca ©2018 except as noted

On the front cover, left to right: Florence Manygoats, Velma Kee Craig, Ailla Teller, Gilbert Nez Begay, Irene Hardy Clark.
Inside covers: Rug woven by Irene Hardy Clark.

THRUMS
B O O K S

306 North Washington Avenue
Loveland, Colorado 80537
USA

Printed in China by Asia Pacific
Library of Congress Control Number: 2018931462

DEDICATION

Barbara: I would like to dedicate this book to my parents, Sam and Ruth Teller; my grandparents, Paul and Nellie Peshlaki Teller; my brothers Ernest Teller Sr. and Earl Teller; and my sisters Rosann Teller Lee and Lynda Teller Pete; my children, Sierra Teller Ornelas and Michael Teller Ornelas; their father, David Ornelas; my grandson, Javier Teller Ornelas O'Mara. Thank you for all your love, support and encouragement. It's been a long journey of weaving. A lot of good and hard times, but we all made it. Like my grandfather used to say, "Hold on to your weaving, my child; it will only bring you love, happiness, and success. Never let it go because weaving will hold your family together."

Lynda: I would like to dedicate this book to my mother, Ruth Teller, my sisters Rosann Teller Lee and Barbara Teller Ornelas, for their leadership, love, support, and encouragement. I would also like to dedicate this book to the tool and loom makers in my family: my father, Sam Teller; my brothers Ernest Teller and Earl Teller; my nephews Larry Lee Jr. and Terry Lee; and my husband, Belvin Pete. Lastly, my love, my North Star, my husband, Belvin Pete, who is on this journey of life with me. Thank you for being my sounding board, for being a nerdy mechanical engineer who brings logic into my whimsical ideas, and for embracing my whole Teller family and elevating our weaving onto a whole new level.

ACKNOWLEDGMENTS

Thank you to Thrums Books, Linda Ligon, Karen Brock, and Joe Coca. Thank you for giving us the opportunity to tell our weaving stories.

Barbara: Thank you, Marilyn Murphy, for inviting me to Tinkuy in Peru where the idea for this book came about. Thank you to Les Wilson from Two Grey Hills Trading Post. Thank you to everyone at the Heard Museum. You took a chance on me when I first started out and still support me today. Thank you to Joe and Cindy Tanner for all your love and support. Thank you to all the weavers who were willing to tell their stories, giving us a small glimpse into their lives.

Lynda: Thank you to all the Navajo weavers who gave generously of their time, shared weaving processes, and shared their stories with me. It was an honor to tell your story. Thank you to the many Navajo weavers who have become good friends and mentors, some of whom are not with us today, but their memories have inspired my weaving and their stories will not be forgotten. Thank you to the younger weavers in my family. Thank you Sierra, Michael, and Roxanne for encouraging me to step outside my boundaries and to weave without constrictions. Thank you to the ever-growing community of fiber friends who have surrounded Barbara and me; I am grateful for their friendships, their support, kindness, and love.

FOREWORD

Every rug tells a story. When my mom and I are together, we often run into one of her weavings. It always happens. We might be window shopping at a Santa Fe art gallery or checking out a museum exhibit or visiting a collector's house. She'll spot her piece and walk over to it. Compelled by the memory it evokes, she'll tell me everything about the rug and what we were going through at the time. ("I had just started dating your dad when I wove that... I got most of the wool from your Grandma Margaret... We used some of the money to go to San Francisco for the first time...") She'll tell me who bought it and if they were fair in the negotiation. She'll point to areas of pattern and explain their significance. ("That dot is you. That one is your brother...")

Some rugs were a respite during lean times, others brought a payday that literally changed the course of our lives. Some rugs took her around the world. I live for these moments, not just with her, but also with my aunt Lynda, my brother Michael, and the other weavers in our family. Each story is a delicate time capsule holding our family's history and the artistic path they've carved out for themselves. It's my family's favorite pastime, sitting in one of our kitchens and "talking shop." One of us will give the play-by-play of a recent sale at an art market or describe how laborious it was to finish a piece. ("That rug almost killed me" is said often.) They'll pitch grand plans for future pieces, inspired by a rug from the 1800s or a recent video game. Weaving is an often obsessive endeavor, and weavers are always working with the next piece on their minds. In the corner of her workroom, my mom also has half-finished rugs, still on the loom, covered with muslin sheets. These tell the stories of weavers who have passed on. She keeps them and holds the hope that she or perhaps a younger generation, one that may not even be born yet, will take them and finish them.

It was during one of these shop talks that my aunt and my mother first told me about their plan to write this book. (To steal one of Aunt Lynda's phrases: Holy buckets! You guys wrote a book!) They explained they'd met Linda Ligon, who has published books on weavers from around the world, and how she was interested in doing one on Navajo weavers. For months, they would come back with stories of traveling the back roads of our Navajo Nation, meeting and visiting fellow weavers. They met elder weavers and listened to their stories. They met weavers in their prime, who spoke of success at marketing their work. But the ones they were most excited to hear from were the young weavers. My mother would say, "They are our future. They will hold our stories. Because of them, Navajo weaving will always be strong and present." My aunt and my mom had a great vision for how they wanted to make this book different from others previously written by non-Navajos and nonweavers. This would be a book by us and for us (though all are, of course, welcome to enjoy). I think they did a great job of capturing the breadth and complexity of who we are and what we do.

When they described their plans, I was immediately reminded of a memory from my past: I was a teenager and my parents drove my brother and me to the Los Angeles County Museum of Art to see a traveling exhibit featuring the painter Vincent van Gogh. I was really excited to see his work in person. The exhibit included detailed text panels describing van Gogh's life, the letters he wrote, and his evolution as an artist. When we were done, my mom noticed that in an adjacent gallery there was an exhibit of Navajo chief's blankets, and she led us in. Woven in the latter parts of the nineteenth century, the blankets towered over us, looming with artistry and color. My mom spent a quiet moment with each one. On the car ride home, she pointed out that the weavers who made those chief's blankets wove them at the same time van Gogh was painting, "and everyone knows who he is, but no one will ever know the names of those weavers." This book aims to put into print what we've known for centuries.

Whenever I look at a rug, I always wonder, who was the person behind the loom? What was she going through when she made it? Was he a caretaker for his family? Was she self-taught? Was he far from home or surrounded by loved ones? Was she in the middle of hard times or her renaissance? Every rug tells a story, and these are ours. I welcome you to take a seat at our kitchen table and listen as these weavers share their histories and those of their families through the medium of my favorite American art form.

Sierra Teller Ornelas

▲ Hesperus Mountain

UTAH
ARIZONA

COLORADO
NEW MEXICO

• Teec Nos Pos Trading Post

• Shiprock   • Farmington
▲ Shiprock

• Red Rock

• Sanostee   • Dzilth-na-o-dith-hle

• Tonalea   • Newcomb
          • Two Grey Hills Trading Post
• Tuba City   • Toadlena Trading Post

          Chinle Canyon   • White Rock
          de Chelly
• Pinon   • Spider Rock   • Crystal

HOPI
RESERVATION   • Tohatchi

          Chuska Peak ▲   • Crownpoint
          • Ganado and Hubbell Trading Post

▲ San Francisco   • Gallup   • Mariano Lake
Peaks   ▲ Mount Taylor

          • Indian Wells

• Leupp
• Flagstaff

COMMUNITIES AND LOCATIONS IN THIS BOOK

In beauty I walk.
With beauty before me I walk.
With beauty behind me I walk.
It is finished in beauty.
With beauty around me I walk.
With beauty below me I walk.
With beauty above and about me I walk.

SPIDER WOMAN

NA'ASHJÉII ASDZÁÁ

AS TOLD BY BARBARA TELLER ORNELAS

In my youth, my brothers, Ernest and Earl Teller, and I were sent to help our paternal grandparents, Paul Kent Teller and Nellie Peshlaki Teller at their homestead in White Rock, New Mexico, during the summers. Their main home had been in the Chuska Mountains, but the Navajo Census came during the time they were at their winter camp, and so that became their main residence.

There, they had a huge flock of sheep, cattle, and horses; and in an otherwise barren and desolate area, they had lush, irrigated spots of greenery and fruit trees. They had a man-made pond for irrigation. My grandmother tended an annual garden and a grove of grapes. My grandfather, originally from Canyon de Chelly, planted and tended fruit trees; he favored the old Canyon peach trees and was known to be a grafter of fruit trees. During these summers, my grandmother taught me about plants and the environment; we dug for gypsum clay to whiten white wool.

In the evenings my brothers and I would get bored, and we would talk about how everyone back at home was probably watching television. Our grandparents would turn on the radio for us, but only for a short while to conserve the batteries. Most often they would set up story time and entertain us—well, entertainment for us, but they were really lesson plans. In the winter when we visited, they did string games with us and told us our creation story. The biggest lesson we learned through their seasonal stories was that everything has a life force; we give respect to the values that each life force, man or animal, has equally.

We learned about *K'é*. K'é is about family, how we treat each other, how we show love, kindness, and generosity to our kin. It is about learning your clans, how to greet and appropriately introduce yourself to other people. At its core, K'é is knowing where you come from, learning language, culture, prayer, songs, and your origin stories. It

SPIDER ROCK, HONORING SPIDER WOMAN, IS AN ARRESTING NATURAL MONUMENT IN CANYON DE CHELLY. PHOTOGRAPH BY VLAD G./SHUTTERSTOCK.COM

was there at our grandparents' hogan that my brothers and I learned our Diné stories, especially about how Spider Woman gave us the gift of weaving.

SPIDER WOMAN

In Navajo tradition, the span of time from the first creation to the present day is composed of five worlds. We live in the current fifth world, "Glittering World." In the emergence from the second world to the third, our Holy People, *Diyin Dine'é*, instructed Spider Woman to weave her pattern of the universe. Then she was to teach the Diné, the Navajo, to weave *Hózhó* (beauty) to bring harmony and beauty into their lives. She had no knowledge of how to do it. But Spider Woman was observant; she watched everything in her environment, and her curiosity focused on a spider weaving a web. This became her plan for how she would weave the universe. When she felt comfortable with her experimental weaving, she returned home and presented it to her husband, Spider Man. With just this basic concept of weaving, the Holy People instructed Spider Woman so that her skills would be further enhanced by prayer, songs, and ceremonial duties.

Spider Woman was told to go to our four sacred mountains to gather specific items to further advance her weaving: Blanca Peak, the sacred mountain of the east, *Sisnaajiní*, "the dawn," or "white shell mountain"; Mount Taylor, the sacred mountain of the south, *Tsoodził*, "turquoise mountain," or "blue bead"; San Francisco Peak, the sacred mountain of the west, *Dook'o'oosłííd*, "the summit which never melts," or "abalone shell mountain"; and Hesperus Mountain, the sacred mountain of the north, *Dibé Nitsaa*, "big sheep." From the first mountain, she got wood for Spider Man to make the loom. From the second mountain, she harvested plants for vegetal colors for her wool. From the third mountain, she got patterns from the thunder gods, from whom she asked permission to use the patterns in her weaving. They granted her permission and told her to learn and teach the patterns so that other weavers could use them. From the last mountain, she got prayers and songs that are associated with all stages of weaving.

Spider Woman began weaving and increased her talents and knowledge about weaving. The Holy People visited her, and with the wood that was gathered, they instructed Spider Man on how to make a weaving loom and how to create the Navajo weaving tools. The top and bottom wood beams were made of sky and earth cords, the tension rods that hold the warps were made of sun rays, the inside heddle and shed rods (we refer to these rods as female and male) were made of rock crystal and sheet lightning. The wood batten was a sun halo to separate the female and male rain warps. The wood weaving comb was made of white shell. There were four spindles: the first spindle of zigzag lightning with a whorl of jet; the second spindle of flash lightning with a whorl of turquoise; the third spindle of sheet lightning with a whorl of abalone; and the fourth spindle a rain streamer with a whorl of white shell.

Later, with our final emergence into "Glittering World," the twin sons of Changing Woman, *Asdzą́ą́ Nádleehé*, went on their journey to find their father, the Sun, *Jóhonaa'éí*. They were near the Spider Rock formation in present day Canyon de Chelly when they noticed a hole in the ground. The twins, Monster-Slayer, *Naayéé' Neizghání*, and Child-Born-of-Water, *Tóbájíshchín*, climbed down and found Spider Woman weaving. By now, Spider woman was fully immersed in weaving, in prayer, in song; she was ready to pass on her gift of weaving. The twins climbed out and with the help of *Haashch'ééłti'í*, Talking God, they took the knowledge of weaving out into the world. We were gifted the art of weaving to keep our families from starving, to be kept in good comfort, and to keep our families together.

Spider Woman is our grandmother, our teacher, our guide, our motivator. We regard our maternal and paternal grandparents as Spider Woman. Our mothers, our aunts, and our sisters, and the weaving men are Spider Woman. Spider Woman instilled fearlessness in some weavers—to take on challenges, to not only weave rugs to provide for their families but to pass on their weaving knowledge.

This is our task.

THIS SMALL RUG BY LYNDA TELLER PETE FEATURES ONE VERSION OF THE SPIDER WOMAN MOTIF, THE CROSSES WITH EXTENSIONS ON THE ARMS IN THE CENTER.

In beauty I walk.

OUR ROOTS

WEAVING IS OUR family legacy. My sister Barbara and I are fifth-generation Navajo weavers from the Newcomb and Two Grey Hills areas of the Navajo Nation. Two Grey Hills is an area in northwest New Mexico, home of the Two Grey Hills Trading Post, more than a century old and one of the few remaining historic posts on the Navajo reservation. Our father, Sam K. Teller, was a trader at this store for more than thirty-five years. His broad wealth of trading post experience, starting at age eleven, and his knowledge of weaving helped sustain and increase the fine reputation that weavers of this region, including our family, gained as these rugs and tapestries became highly collectible and treasured.

We grew up weaving what is known as Two Grey Hills tapestries, taught by our mother, Ruth Teller, and our older sister, Rosann Teller Lee. We continue this weaving tradition with Barbara's two children, Sierra and Michael Ornelas, and her granddaughter, Roxanne Lee, all of whom you'll hear more about later in this book.

Our family, the Teller family, is but one Navajo weaving family out of thousands in the Navajo Nation, and each family does things a little differently. There are multiple regional and historical period styles; these can be mixed with contemporary pop culture, abstract styles, and more.

A MASSIVE STONE MESA RISING FROM THE VALLEY FLOOR ECHOES THE COLORS AND MOTIFS OF TWO GREY HILLS RUGS.

We see these fusions showing up in the various generations in our own family. Barbara and I have become the torchbearers in our family since our grandmothers, our mother, and our best teacher, our sister Rosann, have passed. It is up to us to influence, inspire, and educate our family with our weaving traditions. Like us, many Navajo weaving families have their own traditions and knowledge passed down from elders.

For seven generations, our grandmothers, mother, sisters, aunts, cousins, nieces, and nephews have produced rugs and tapestries of the highest quality. Our extended Newcomb-area family is known for weaving rugs in the traditional Two Grey Hills pattern. Identified primarily by a double-diamond layout and intricate geometric designs using natural-colored, handcarded and handspun wool, these rugs are easily recognizable. These finely woven rugs are known for their high weft counts. To qualify as a true Two Grey Hills tapestry today, the weft count has to be above 80 in a one-inch-square measurement, an intricate calculation that takes into account the number of pattern blocks and different weights of handspun yarn as well as the fineness of the weave. In addition to this fine weave, our family uses a trademark rich brown wool for the inside color field.

In our family, we regard weaving as our life's work; weaving represents our connection to the universe. It is our stories, our prayers, and our songs, told, chanted, sung, and preserved in the weaving motions. All Navajo weavers have stories to tell about their weaving, and every weaving has stories to tell about the weaver.

RUTH SHORTY BEGAY TELLER

NEWCOMB, NEW MEXICO

BORN TO THE WATER'S EDGE CLAN, *Tábąąhá*

BORN FOR RED BOTTOM PEOPLE, *Tł'ááshchí'í*

MOTHER'S FATHER, MANY HOGANS CLAN, *Hooghan Łání*

FATHER'S FATHER, ONE-WALKS-AROUND CLAN, *Honágháahnii*

Ruth Shorty Begay Teller was our mother, born to Susie Tom and James Shorty Begay of Newcomb, New Mexico. Her older sister was Marie Shorty Begay Joe, and Margaret Shorty Begay Yazzie was her younger sister. She had four half-siblings: three brothers and her sister, Mary Louise Tom Gould. Our mother passed on in November 2014, at age eighty-seven. She lived her entire life in the Newcomb area. [she also lived at Two Grey Hills, see next page] She was a fourth-generation master weaver of the Two Grey Hills style.

She learned how to do basic weaving from her older sister Marie in the mid-1930s, but she would go with her mother, Susie, to other area weavers' houses, where she loved seeing all the dyed wool. She couldn't wait to learn how to dye and weave with these bright colors—reds, yellows, greens, and shades of blue. But when it came time to weave her first rug, she was told that the only colors she could use were the natural black, white, gray, and blended tans, and our family's special natural reddish brown. These color restrictions came as directives from the traders at Newcomb and Two Grey Hills Trading Posts.

THIS PHOTO OF RUTH TELLER WAS TAKEN IN THE 1960S. THE RUG IN THE BACKGROUND IS AN EXAMPLE OF HER TRADITIONAL TWO GREY HILLS STYLE.

By late 1945, our mother was married to Sam Teller and living with our paternal grandparents in White Rock, New Mexico, near Burnham. Her mother-in-law, Nellie Peshlaki Teller, originally from the Two Grey Hills/Toadlena, New Mexico, area, wove saddle blankets and knew many twill patterns and two-face weaving. She also wove a lot of pictorial designs, getting her inspiration from gum wrappers, baking powder cans, and store logos. Our mother learned a lot more about weaving from her mother-in-law: how to warp effectively, how to plan her designs, and how to troubleshoot myriad challenging weaving issues. Our mother already knew all the tricks of the trade of the finishing process—weaving the last tight, critical inches of a piece—from her years of watching her mother perform this special skill for other weavers. Her father-in-law, Paul Teller, was from Canyon del Muerto inside Canyon de Chelly, Arizona, and he taught her the songs and prayers associated with weaving.

When my father returned from serving in the Army after World War II, my parents settled in Two Grey Hills, where he got a job at the Two Grey Hills Trading Post. They raised five children: Rosann, Ernest, Barbara, Earl, and me (Lynda) and lived seasonally at the trading post. This is where our mother learned the marketing of rugs, kept up with current trends of weaving styles, met other weavers, and exchanged weaving stories. When tourists came to the post, our mother demonstrated weaving. She wove a lot of Two Grey Hills tapestries, but she is not noted in weaving books nor was she interviewed by textile scholars because her work was not in art shows or galleries, or even at other area trading posts.

NELLIE PESHLAKI TELLER, PHOTOGRAPHED IN 1960, WOVE A VARIETY OF STYLES: TWO GREY HILLS, PICTORIALS, TWILLS, AND THE CHALLENGING TWO-FACED TECHNIQUE. SHE WAS THE AUTHORS' PATERNAL GRANDMOTHER.

When the tourists came to see her, they often bought her rugs right off the loom. As children, we would get packages from all over the world with newspaper clippings or other publications from Germany, Japan, England, and other far-away places with photos of our mother and the rug she had sold. We couldn't read the articles because they were in foreign languages.

Little did we know that our mother was also learning English during her demonstrations, and we could no longer keep things from her as teenagers, which I guess is not a bad thing. She developed a keen interest in recording the legacies of area weavers by taking photographs of their work. She always had a camera slung around her neck and she took a lot of photos of her own work and her family's work. I asked her about her mother Susie Tom's weavings when we looked through her books of photos and saw several rugs that had feathers woven in. My mother said that they would go to a medicine man for healing ceremonies where her mother saw the medicine man make a feather dance without aid of his hands, strings, or any hidden devices. Her mother said that medicine was very powerful and she wove the feathers in her rugs to honor the medicine man and his healing. I went through boxes of old photos with her and she told me who the weaver was, whether they were her weavings, or her mother's, or her sisters'.

I kept seeing some designs over and over in her weaving and I asked her why she used her mother's or her grandmother's designs. "I miss them," she said. "I miss their voices, I miss hearing the beating of their combs. I use their designs to feel their presence."

Our mother gave up weaving around 1998 and picked up hand quilting and other less taxing fabric arts to remain productive. In 2010, after she had had a lengthy hospital stay, Barbara and I gave her a little Japanese plastic loom to cheer her up. We gave her commercially processed and dyed wool from our weaving classes and she did cheer up,

SUSIE TOM WAS THE MOTHER OF RUTH SHORTY BEGAY TELLER, MATERNAL GRANDMOTHER OF THE AUTHORS. NOTE HOW FINE HER WEAVING COMB IS.

adjusted the plastic loom to Navajo style, and started weaving small rugs with blasts of color and bold designs, hardly stopping to eat, sleep, or rest. Our mother was finally weaving with brightly colored wool! She made so many little rugs that I created a Facebook page for her and sold her rugs, which delighted her.

She was so proud of our weaving achievements, Barbara, Sierra, Michael, Roxanne, and me. She would ask about each weaver after our art shows, she collected the magazines and books that we were featured in, and she asked for photos.

NELLIE PASHKELI WOVEN SAMPLERS TO HELP VISITING CUSTOMERS CHOOSE DESIGNS. THE TOP SAMPLER INCLUDES SEVERAL TWILLS, AND ESPECIALLY THE TWO-FACED WEAVING SHE MASTERED.

THIS IS THE LAST RUG WOVEN BY THE AUTHORS' MOTHER, RUTH. IT LACKS THE USUAL WEAVER'S PATH WHICH LEADS TO THE NEXT WEAVING, AS SHE KNEW THIS WOULD BE HER LAST.

Every weaver in my family has stories of strength, of re-siliency, of determination, and my mother was the strongest person I knew. From her, we are living in balance, we are singing the songs, and we are doing our prayers. We may add our own variations here and there, but the weaving lineage is strong in each of us.

RIGHT: TOO OLD TO MANAGE A FULL-SIZED LOOM, RUTH TELLER DELIGHTED IN WEAVING SMALL, BRIGHTLY COLORED SAMPLES, WHICH HER DAUGHTERS SOLD ONLINE.

THE RUG BELOW WAS WOVEN BY SUSIE TOM WHEN SHE WAS IN HER SEVENTIES, FOLLOWING CHEMOTHERAPY AND OTHER HEALTH PROBLEMS. EVEN SO, SHE INCLUDED A WEAVER'S PATH (UPPER RIGHT) TO LEAD HER TO HER NEXT WORK.

MARGARET YAZZIE

NEWCOMB, NEW MEXICO

BORN TO THE WATER'S EDGE CLAN, *Tábąąhá*

BORN FOR RED BOTTOM PEOPLE, *Tł'ááshchí'í*

MOTHER'S FATHER, MANY HOGANS CLAN, *Hooghan Łání*

FATHER'S FATHER, ONE-WALKS-AROUND CLAN, *Honágháahnii*

Margaret Shorty Begay Yazzie is our maternal aunt, the younger sister of our mother, Ruth Shorty Begay Teller. She is eighty-eight years old. Their third sister was Marie Shorty Begay Joe; she was the oldest of the three sisters. Their parents were Susie and James Shorty Begay of Newcomb, New Mexico. Her mother, her grandmother, and her great-grandmother were all weavers. When Margaret, Ruth, and Marie were young, their mother, Susie, was known in the area to finish weavers' rugs. When she was hired, she would take the girls with her and they helped her with the finishing process. This involved weaving in the last few inches when the warp is very tight, maintaining tension and pattern, as well as troubleshooting any edge or tension problems.

Margaret lost her father at a young age. Her mother, Susie, in order to provide for the family, remarried, a second arranged marriage. With the new marriage, there was a second set of siblings and Margaret, Marie, and Ruth were placed with either their grandmother, Diné łitso Bitsi, who lived near the old Newcomb Trading Post which was located by the roadside of Highway 491, or with their maternal aunts, Lelia Yazzie or Josephine Gould, to help out with farm chores and

MARGARET LIVES SURROUNDED BY HER TOOLS, PAST WEAVINGS, AND FAMILY PHOTOGRAPHS.

MARGARET'S SON, JONES, WAS A CASUALTY OF THE VIETNAM WAR, BUT HIS MEMORY IS STRONG IN GALLERY OF FAMILY PHOTOS THAT GRACE MARGARET'S WALLS.

with herding sheep.

During her sheepherding chores, Margaret picked off wool that was in the bushes and when she had a boxful, she taught herself how to card the wool. She was amazed at the color blending. She didn't stop at blending two colors, like black and white to make a grayish black. When she achieved a bright white, she slowly mixed in other blended grays to get a bluish tint.

Margaret remembers weaving her first rug but doesn't remember where it got sold; a clue would be that her grandmother was very loyal to the Newcomb Trading Post, so this

WHEN A WEAVER FINISHES A RUG, SHE IS USUALLY QUICK TO START ANOTHER, PREPARING A WARP AND WEAVING THE FIRST FEW WEFT PASSES. THEN IT WILL BE READY FOR HER WHEN SHE IS ABLE TO SIT AT THE LOOM AGAIN.

may be where her rug was sold. The Livestock Reduction described on page 55 also affected the area families and was a very painful chapter in their family's history. She remembers the frantic butchering and having to find places to dry the meat. The girls were briefly placed at the Toadlena Boarding School when there were no more herding chores; Margaret had at most two years of schooling. Early on, Margaret watched her mother weave, and as she lived with her aunts and mostly with her grandmother, she watched them weave as well. She took note that they all had different weaving techniques, different ways of solving weaving problems, setting the path for her supreme troubleshooting skills and knowledge for which she was later sought out by area weavers for assistance.

Margaret was the youngest of the three girls but the first to be in an arranged marriage—to Wilson Yazzie. They had nine children, with seven surviving: Paul, Sarah, Lula, Gilbert, Ramona, Melvin, and Gladys. Margaret is a Gold Star mother; she lost her second oldest son, Jones, a self-enlisted lance corporal in the United States Marines, in Vietnam.

As her family grew, Margaret acquired her own flock of sheep and returned to weaving, to supplement her husband's income.

Margaret was a hardworking woman. Clad in her Navajo traditional velvet blouse and three-tiered skirt with her long black hair tied up in a *tsiiyééł*, the Navajo hair bun, she could be seen lambing, tossing hay, driving through cornfields for leftover cornstalks to feed her sheep. Wilson worked seasonally as a laborer on the railroad in various states, leaving home for long stretches of time. Wilson bought a vehicle and had a co-worker drive him to the family's home in Newcomb, intending to learn how to drive so he could come home more often. However, it was Margaret who immediately learned how to drive, giving her more independence. When she was eighty-eight, her children asked her to drive only on the dirt roads to go to the Newcomb Chapter House or to church. The sorrow in her voice at her limited driving was heartbreaking.

Margaret has had an illustrious weaving career, winning a lot of awards from regional art shows such as the Gallup Inter-Tribal Ceremonial. One of her masterpiece Two Grey Hills tapestries, woven in 1981, is part of the Santa Fe Collection of Charles and Linda Rimmer. The collection was acquired by the Heard Museum and is now part of its permanent collection. Margaret's work has been photographed for many publications, including *Navajo Weaving in the Late Twentieth Century: Kin, Community, and Collectors* by Dr. Ann Hedlund. Dr. Arch Gould, an important collector from Utah, bought all of her work in the latter part of Margaret's weaving career, providing her, our mother Ruth, and our aunt Mary Louise with a steady quarterly supplemental income in return for whatever tapestries they wove.

THIS UNFINISHED PIECE SHOWS THE FINENESS AND CLOSE SETT OF THE WARP, AND THE LOVELY NATURAL SHEEP COLORS. MARGARET ACCOMPLISHES THE BLUISH GRAY BY CAREFULLY BLENDING SHADES OF GRAY AND WHITE.

MARY LOUISE GOULD

NEWCOMB, NEW MEXICO

BORN TO THE WATER'S EDGE CLAN, *Tábąąhá*

BORN FOR THE WATER-FLOWS-TOGETHER CLAN, *Tó'aheedlíinii*

MOTHER'S FATHER, MANY HOGANS CLAN, *Hooghan Łání*

FATHER'S FATHER, MUD CLAN, *Hashtł'ishnii*

Mary Louise Tom Gould is our maternal aunt and is eighty-two years old. Mary Louise is half- sister to our mother Ruth and our Aunt Margaret. She and my uncles Amos, Alvin, and Raymond are the children by our grandmother, Susie, and Albert Tom of Newcomb. Mary Louise attended schools in Newcomb and in Phoenix, Arizona. She was the babysitter for our older brother, Ernest. There are a lot of photos of the two of them; in some, Mary Louise is in traditional Navajo dress, tiered skirt, and silver coin-lined velvet shirt, but she is sporting a short haircut with curls instead of the traditional Navajo bun, and white Keds instead of moccasins. They are certainly glamour shots!

In 1954, Mary Louise entered an arranged marriage to Arthur Gould, a Korean War veteran, and they raised Laverne, Laphine, Irving, Lenora, and Lorraine in Newcomb. Mary Louise learned how to card, spin, and weave from her mother in the traditional Two Grey Hills style. Her daughter Lorraine says that there was a seasonal cycle to their weaving: summer projects were done for buying school clothes; fall projects done for the Northern Navajo Nation Fair in Shiprock, New Mexico; winter projects done in time for Christmas; and spring projects done for food. The girls are now all adults, raising their families; some are full-time weavers, some weave part-time, and some are teaching their children.

When I was in high school, Mary Louise would come to my mother's house and talk about her flock of sheep and how she tried to breed the sheep to get the highly coveted reddish brown that is our family's signature inside field color in our Two Grey Hills tapestries. Several years later, she succeeded and at one point, she had a large flock of sheep. In 2012, her flock had dwindled down to only seventy-five, and by 2017, she had only four sheep left. However, she has a stockpile of clean skirted fleece, carded rolags ready to be spun, pencil roving all in boxes, and boxes of various colors and blended colors: reddish brown in every shade, natural black, aniline-dyed black, natural cream white, gypsum whitened white, several shades of gray from light to dark, and the same with tan and brown.

Mary Louise has found inspiration in the work and techniques of her large community and her close-knit family members, all weaving the Two Grey Hills style, but late in life she has developed her own distinctive style that has catapulted her into master weaver status. In her seventies, Mary Louise wanted to weave something different, get out of her Two Grey Hills style. She did a borderless Chinle style with bands and intricate geometric designs that repeated. She took it to a local trading post and the trader took one look at it and said to her, "Are you crazy?" She was deeply hurt and

A LARGE STASH OF PREPARED SPINNING FIBERS ARE THE REMAINS OF WHAT WAS ONCE A LARGE FLOCK OF SHEEP, NOW DWINDLED TO FOUR.

slowed down her weaving. When Barbara and I visited her, we told her, "You have nothing to prove anymore, you are a master weaver; you can weave whatever you want. Gone are the days of being pigeonholed into a regional style; someone will like your tapestry and buy it." Later, our cousin Lorraine sent us a note. "Thank you for lifting our mother's spirit and we are all pleased to see her smiling and being in her work-room again. You have really motivated her." You can't keep a master weaver down too long.

Accolades, awards, and ribbons have piled up. Her grand-daughter Stacey said she drove her grandmother to the Wheelwright Museum in Santa Fe, where a tapestry of hers was on exhibit. When they arrived, Stacey said she was in awe of her grandmother's work and utterly flabbergasted that there were so many fans of her grandmother in attendance.

The power of her reputation is reflected in the prices she now can command. She negotiated a commission to weave a very large Two Grey Hills tapestry for a new casino and received twenty-five percent of the agreed-on price. She fin-ished it, but the casino wanted to renegotiate. Undaunted, she took her tapestry to Richardson's Trading Post in Gallup, New Mexico, sold it, gave the casino back its down-payment percentage, and drove away in her brand-new pickup truck. That's how we roll in our community!

With beauty before me I walk.

TWO GREY HILLS

GROWING UP AS a "trading post kid," I have nostalgic feelings for the past glory days, for the hustle and bustle of a thriving post. Watching Navajo families that came to buy, trade, or sell, but mostly to visit, became a favorite pastime of mine. The most exciting days were when the busloads of tourists came to the post: trying to figure out where they were from by their accents or clothing, watching my father wrapping up rugs in brown butcher paper and tying them with cotton strings. If a high-weft-count tapestry was sold, he was careful to pad the package with more paper.

If my sister Rosann took her tapestries to other area trading posts, she was greeted and offered coffee, but after small talk pleasantries were exchanged, the tone changed: determination by Rosann and apprehension by the trader. It was choreographed like a dance with Rosann taking the lead. That was my school. I learned that I love marketing rugs and tapestries, and I also learned that I hated marketing my own. Now I am more confident; I have improved my weaving skills, and I channel my sister Rosann's marketing style.

In past generations, trading posts had tremendous influence over weavers' lives and what they wove. They bought rugs in

LES WILSON AND IRMA HENDERSON HAVE RUN THE TWO GREY HILLS TRADING POST SINCE 1983. IRMA, WHO MANAGES THE LIVESTOCK, HAS KEPT HER FAMILY NAME OUT OF RESPECT FOR THE MATRILINEAL NATURE OF NAVAJO TRADITIONAL CULTURE.

return for money or groceries and supplies or a combination of both. They used their market knowledge to dictate what style of rug they would buy, as in the case of Two Grey Hills weavers being limited for many years to using only natural wool colors. They pushed weavers to higher levels of excellence. They were often accused of exploiting the weavers.

I have visited several historic posts over the past few years and have seen that they are no longer the places they once were. Some still have rugs and tapestries, but many are little more than convenience stores for people in the area. One big positive difference I have noticed at the posts that still deal in rugs is that most of them now attach name tags to the weavings, some even with photos. This is a big change from the days of the unknown weaver.

I imagine it is hard to make a post profitable now with all

ABOVE: IRMA HAS A STRONG AFFINITY FOR THE BURROS AND SHEEP AT THE POST.

OPPOSITE TOP: THE RUG ROOM AT TWO GREY HILLS CONTAINS A TREASURE OF HIGH QUALITY RUGS.

OPPOSITE BELOW: NAVAJO-MADE GOODS FOR TOURISTS, DAILY ESSENTIALS AND WEAVING SUPPLIES FOR NEARBY RESIDENTS —AN ACTIVE TRADING POST SERVES MANY NEEDS.

the competition from retailers and craft dealers in the nearby towns. I am grateful that I grew up with my siblings at the Two Grey Hills Trading Post, one that continues to thrive. It made me a curious person and gave me a yen to travel to places where the tourists came from. And it supports our traditions.

Here are the stories of weavers you might meet if you visit the trading post today.

REGINA CHARLEY

TWO GREY HILLS, NEW MEXICO

BORN TO THE MUD CLAN, *Hashtł'ishnii*

BORN FOR THE MEXICAN PEOPLE CLAN, *Naakaii Dine'é*

MOTHER'S FATHER, SLEEP ROCK PEOPLE CLAN, *Tse'Na'Bllithni*

FATHER'S FATHER, BITTER WATER CLAN, *Tódích'íi'nii*

Regina is a full-time Navajo legacy weaver, which means that both her mother and her grandmother on both sides of her family were master weavers. Her mother is Rena Charley and her maternal grandmother is Helen Shorty Begay, both of whom specialized in the Two Grey Hills style. Regina's father is Henry Charley; her paternal grandmother is Mary Charley. Regina has two older sisters, Marlene and Karlene. Marlene passed away in 2016, leaving behind her five-year-old daughter, Valerie Yazzie, and Karlene lives and works in Grants, New Mexico. In all families, losing family members, young and old, is part of life and there is no shortage of grief on the Navajo Nation when it comes to losing family members.

Regina is married to Alfred Johnhat, and in all our interviews about commuting to jobs outside the Navajo Nation borders, Alfred gets the award for the longest commute. He travels to Florida for employment, leaving Regina to maintain home and school life for their two sons, Ryan, seventeen, and Alex, ten.

Regina learned how to weave watching her grandmothers, mother, and her two older sisters. She wove her first rug

LEFT: THIS FINELY WOVEN TAPESTRY USES THE CHALLENGING "ONE WARP" TECHNIQUE DESCRIBED ON PAGE 37.

when she was in grade school and gave it to her older sister Marlene. After getting more lessons, she took her second rug to Les Wilson at the Two Grey Hills Trading Post. Her mother and her sister Marlene prepped her for the sale: be confident, be ready to talk about what you learned on your second rug, and how much money to ask for, and speak up! She was confident on their drive to the post. But once she got face-to-face with the trader, she became very shy and nervous and completely blanked out all the earlier prepping and looked to her mom to help her with the negotiation. She cannot remember how much she received or what she did with her money.

In later years, she tried selling her rugs elsewhere, but was daunted by the harsh criticism of perceived weaving errors. She said that when you are weaving in a house full of weavers, someone will always point out your weaving errors, so she decided to only take her rugs to the Two Grey Hills Trading Post.

When she was twenty-five, Regina hit upon a design theme of a stacked diagonal pattern that her mother said looked like spiders. This signature "spider design" became a best-seller. She weaves a variety of sizes, from small to large, and most often, it's the small to medium sizes that sell the fastest. Les Wilson remarked that for the new generation of Navajo

BELOW AND PREVIOUS PAGE: DIAGONAL LINES OF STACKED "STAIR STEPS" ARE REGINA'S SIGNATURE PATTERN.

weavers from the Two Grey Hills, Toadlena, and Newcomb communities, he regarded Regina's sister Marlene as the best of the best weavers in her age group, but with Marlene's passing, Regina's rugs are now the best-selling that he handles.

Regina uses commercial warp and commercially processed wool from the Brown Sheep Company in sport weight, but

When she was twenty-five, Regina hit upon a design theme of a stacked diagonal pattern that her mother said looked like spiders. This signature "spider design" became a best-seller.

she often has to re-spin to get the yarns fine enough and uniform in size. Most rugs today with geometric designs use a two-warp design block, meaning the pattern weft goes over one warp and under the next before returning on the next pass. Because Regina re-spins the commercial weft wool to such a fine grist, she started weaving one-warp designs, a weaving technique that requires expert weaving skills. The one-warp designs are in her borders and inside her design motifs, giving the overall rug fine, well-defined design outlines. It takes her three weeks to a month to weave one of her smaller rugs.

Regina's grandmothers, grandfathers, mother, father, and her sister Marlene have passed, and coping with the losses of her cherished grandfathers, weaving teachers, mentors, supporters and a sibling has been overwhelming at times but has also shaped her resolve to keep weaving. Through the stages of past and very recent grief, Regina has put herself fully into her weaving. She said, "I will keep weaving in loving memory of my family members." Regina will continue to weave the Two Grey Hills style, to honor the legacy of her grandmothers, her mother, and her sister Marlene.

LOSS OF A SISTER, CARE OF HER SONS, AND KEEPING THE HOME FIRES BURNING DURING HER HUSBAND'S ABSENCE BECAUSE OF A FAR DISTANT JOB OCCUPY THE ATTENTION OF THIS SKILLED, DEDICATED WEAVER.

SHIRLEY BROWN

TOADLENA AND TWO GREY HILLS, NEW MEXICO

BORN TO THE COYOTE PASS PEOPLE, *Mąʼii Deeshgiizhinii*

Shirley and her sister, Bernice Tsosie, grew up in Toadlena, New Mexico. Rose Tsosie and George Benally are their parents. Her maternal grandmother was master weaver Mattie Naakaii Tsosie. In the three closely connected communities of Two Grey Hills, Newcomb, and Toadlena, there are many Navajo weaving families. At a community meeting, bumping into unassuming master weavers and other weavers on their career paths to master level is common. I imagine if one were to attend a family event at Shirley's homestead, the scene would be similar.

Shirley's family is filled with renowned master weavers, and she is on the same path with some modern challenges. Shirley learned how to weave from her mother and from watching her grandmother. At Newcomb High School, she also studied with influential teacher Rose Blueeyes, whose family lineage is also heavy with master weavers of the Two Grey Hills style. After high school, Shirley married, put weaving aside, and gave birth to her daughter, Ashley, and three sons. However, she raised them as a single mother, and that precipitated her decision to start weaving again.

Shirley works at the Two Grey Hills Trading Post and supplements her income with her weaving. With wool roving available at the store, she has taught herself how to spin. Irma Henderson, Les Wilson's wife, tried to teach her how to use

ONE OF SHIRLEY'S MASTERPIECES, THIS LARGE RUG USES TWO SHADES OF RED WHICH SHE DYES HERSELF, ALONG WITH WHITE, NATURAL GRAY, AND BLACK.

a spinning wheel but it did not appeal to her as much as a Navajo lap spindle, which she uses exclusively.

Shirley became interested in the Post's history, especially during the time period of Willard Leighton, 1946 to 1959, when he brought in dyes and encouraged area weavers to dye wool in shades of turquoise. These hues, including sky blue, light blue, blue with a touch of gray, and bright to muted turquoise to aqua, particularly intrigued Shirley. She took some white commercial Brown Sheep wool skeins and dyed them

SHIRLEY DYES COMMERCIAL YARN TO THE PRECISE SHADE OF BLUE SHE LIKES AS AN ACCENT IN HER TWO GREY HILLS RUGS. THE USE OF COLOR ACCENTS DATES BACK TO THE DAYS WHEN WILLARD LEIGHTON OWNED THE TRADING POST.

with Cushing dye, a union dye that will color wool as well as cotton. Now she often weaves the dyed wool in as an accent and says it looks as if her Two Grey Hills style has a turquoise squash blossom necklace.

ABOVE: THE VIVID COLORS, BOLD GEOMETRICS, AND ELABORATE BORDERS OF THIS RUG SUGGEST TEEC NOS POS STYLE.

BELOW RIGHT: SHIRLEY'S DAUGHTER, ASHLEY, PREFERS TO WEAVE IN THE RELATIVE CALM OF THE TRADING POST, RATHER THAN IN HER BUSY HOUSEHOLD.

ASHLEY TSOSIE

TOADLENA AND TWO GREY HILLS, NEW MEXICO

BORN TO THE COYOTE PASS PEOPLE, *Mą'ii Deeshgiizhinii*

Shirley's daughter, Ashley, is married to Garrith Bitsilly and they have two children, a nine-year-old son and two-year-old daughter, Tiana. The new normal for residents of the Navajo Nation is to commute to nearby towns for employment, and sometimes not-so-nearby towns; in fact, Garrith commutes 240 miles round trip to Durango, Colorado, from Tuesday to Saturday. He's at home for just Sunday and Monday, while Ashley works at the Two Grey Hills Trading Post from Monday to Saturday. Needless to say, Ashley has single-

She doesn't draw her designs out; she sits at her loom and surprisingly, she often weaves designs used by her mother and grandmother.

parent duties during the week and is unable to weave at home. When she comes to work at the Post, she uses the quiet times to weave and offers demonstrations to the many tourists that flock there year-round.

Ashley learned to weave when she was a teenager, watching her mother, Shirley, and her grandmother, Rose Tsosie. But when she attended Newcomb High School, for fun she enrolled in Rose Blueeyes's weaving class (the same woman who taught her mother), thinking it would be an easy "A." It was not. However, she learned to refine her techniques, and she took additional lessons from another teacher, Mrs. Thomas. Ashley says she was lucky to have had many weaving teachers and it has made her a better weaver.

When she was seventeen, she wove her first rug, a Two Grey Hills, and sold it to Les Wilson at the Post for 80 dollars. She tried taking her rugs to other posts, but the criticism she endured made her question her ability to weave. So she took the unsold rugs to the Two Grey Hills Trading Post, where they sold easily. To this day, this is her only outlet for her rug sales—and her rugs do sell.

Les and his wife, Irma, stock the store with roving, which Ashley uses to spin some of her wool. She mixes the handspun with Brown Sheep Company sport-weight wool, which she respins to get a finer weight. The many rugs that are brought to the store by weavers inspire her. She doesn't draw her designs out; she sits at her loom and surprisingly, she often weaves designs used by her mother and grandmother. But, of course, she incorporates her own designs to complement the family's signature elements. Like her mother, Shirley, Ashley sometimes weaves with turquoise blue dyed weft in her Two Grey Hills rugs. Shirley and Ashley's signature style of using the turquoise blue that was started in the era of Willard Leighton in the 1950s, long before both mother and daughter were born, is a true testament that history repeats itself. And in this context, it's a wonderful homage.

RESPUN COMMERCIAL YARN ALLOWS ASHLEY TO ACHIEVE HIGH WEFT COUNTS AND CRISP DESIGNS.

With beauty behind me I walk.

ELDER MASTERS

SPIDER WOMAN IS THE central figure of our Diyin Dine'é (Holy People). She was instructed to weave the universe. She worked beyond her capabilities, discovering talents, drawing from unknown stamina until she had woven a map of the universe and the patterns of stars in the night sky. She gave us the gift of Navajo weaving. Each weaver displays the qualities of Spider Woman—her determination, her knowledge, her skill. She is our teacher and guide and inspires weavers to keep improving. Spider Woman instilled the determination in some weavers to be fearless, to take on challenges, to not only weave rugs to provide for their families but to weave as a way to pass on knowledge, knowledge of sacred beings and animals.

Elder master weavers across the Navajo Nation are still weaving and still sharing the gifts of Spider Woman with the younger generations. Even as age limits their capacity for doing the heavy physical work required to produce their masterpieces, they have accepted these limitations. They have adapted. They weave a new path by sometimes using commercially processed wool weft and wool warp to continue their work. They may have to rely on a younger family member to help warp their looms. But still they weave, because Spider Woman's strength is their legacy. Our elders, through endurance, defiance, and resilience, continue to pass on the living knowledge of our people. Navajo weavers must preserve, teach, and honor our weaving traditions to keep them alive. This is our story.

IRENE HARDY CLARK

CRYSTAL, NEW MEXICO

BORN OF THE WATER'S EDGE CLAN, *Tábąąhá*

BORN FOR ONE-WALKS-AROUND CLAN, *Honágháahnii*

Irene was born in 1934 and raised in Crystal, New Mexico. Her mother was master weaver Glenabah Hardy; Irene weaves in the same Crystal style as her mother and grandmother. Irene didn't start weaving at an early age. Instead, she herded the family's flock of sheep. But when she returned the sheep to the corral, she would watch her mother weave, and these visual lessons stayed with her.

Irene attended Chilocco Indian School in Oklahoma, where she met her husband, Jimmy. When she returned home, she finally began weaving. For her first rug, she asked her mother to just watch her and to point out weaving errors. With no hands-on lessons, she had basically taught herself by watching, listening, and figuring out the challenges her grandmother and her mother encountered in their weaving. She sold her first rug to a trading post for 400 dollars.

Irene learned the traditional way of weaving, first preparing her materials, carding, spinning, collecting plants for dyeing. Finally, with the proper Navajo weaving songs, she would start weaving. Songs, prayers, and good thoughts are associated with every step of her weaving. She is mindful that each rug has to be finished, each rug teaches her something new, and she never leaves her loom empty for too long.

Irene said, "I do my blessing before each rug. I thank Mother Earth for the plants that give color to my wool, for the sky above me, the air I breathe, for mother earth for grounding me. All this gives me a good feeling to weave." Irene explains,

"Everything is in the weaving, it's in your hands, it's in your weaving tools, and it's in your mind. Design and dyeing are related to how you think of yourself, and it will show in how you weave your rug. Good thoughts, prayers, songs are what you need." Irene's rugs tell her stories; some tell of her struggles to succeed, but all tell of her connection to the harvested plants that provided the beautiful dyes for which she is known. Dyeing is in her family.

Irene's mother, Glenabah, was known for a particular design she often wove in her Crystal rugs—two inverted triangles with a square in the middle of the triangles, a design that would please algebra and geometry teachers. The design element represents a tsiiyéél, the hair bun worn by Navajos. After her mother passed, Irene has continued to weave this design to honor her mother.

Irene is a well-traveled weaver. We first met in 1992 at the opening of *Reflections of the Weaver's World: The Gloria F. Ross Collection of Contemporary Navajo Weaving* at the Denver Art Museum. As the exhibit traveled, we met in museums in other cities, the most memorable being the George Gustav Heye Center in New York. Irene wore Navajo clothing and her jewelry was beautiful. The rotunda at the Heye Center was filled with Navajo weavers, many in their most elegant clothing, and you could hear the Navajo language bouncing off the walls, creating an echo that sounded like songs. After meeting Irene many times at different Navajo weaving events, we finally had quality time to talk about

OPPOSITE: IRENE'S CLOSE CONNECTION TO THE LAND AND HER TRADITIONS SHOW IN THE WISDOM OF HER FACE.

IRENE'S RUGS ARE IN HARMONY WITH THE LANDSCAPE AND THE RHYTHM OF LIFE.

weaving when we both attended the Navajo Weaving Now! conference in Tucson in 2005. We are of the same clan, Water's Edge Clan, *Tábąąhá*, so we are related; after we talked about our weaving, we became family.

Irene's weaving accolades are many, but the ribbons for those countless weaving career achievements she tucks away. Still humble about her work, Irene says, "My current rug always teaches me something new; I am going to challenge myself to do better." Because she has this relationship with each rug she weaves, Irene feels like she has given a piece of herself away when she sells a rug, having put so much of herself in the weaving. Sometimes she even misses a rug after she sells it.

Irene also has been an important weaving teacher—it is one of the many ways she has passed on the heart of her Navajo traditions. She encourages her students to remember their prayers and their songs. "We are carrying on the Holy Ones' work," she reminds them. Irene is a weaver who honors the Holy Ones and Spider Woman in all her work and in all her words.

LEFT AND BELOW: IRENE COLLECTS DYE MATERIALS AS SHE WALKS ACROSS HER LAND. SAGE, LICHENS, AND BLUE CORN ARE AMONG THE DYESTUFFS SHE USES. LIKE HER GREAT-GRANDMOTHER, SHE USES AN ALUM MORDANT IN HER DYEPOTS.

OPPOSITE: THIS STRIKING RUG IS IN THE TYPICAL CRYSTAL STYLE, WITH NATURAL DYES, PATTERNED STRIPES, AND NO BORDERS.

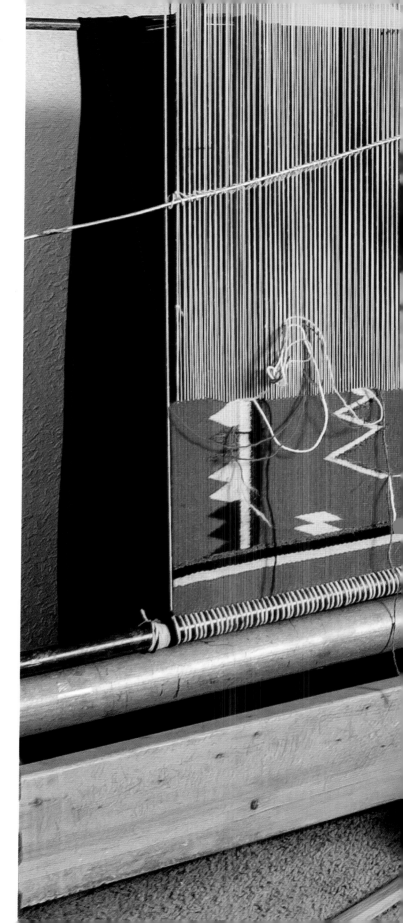

RENA BEGAY

PIÑON, ARIZONA

BORN OF THE TANGLE PEOPLE, *Ta'neeszahnii*

BORN FOR THE BITTER WATER CLAN, *Tódích'íi'nii*

MOTHER'S FATHER, RED-RUNNING-INTO-THE-WATER PEOPLE, *Táchii'nii*

FATHER'S FATHER, COYOTE PASS JEMEZ CLAN, *Ma'íí deeshgíízhíníí*

Rena and Henry Begay live in a modern hogan near Piñon, Arizona, to the west of Chinle and Canyon de Chelly. They entered an arranged marriage set up by their parents in 1957. The arrangement did not go smoothly; Rena laughingly says, "We had a shaky start." When her parents informed her that she would be married at age seventeen, Rena refused. Instead, she started weaving. Henry and Rena met at the Piñon Trading Post later in the year and eventually he was able to convince Rena to be a couple. They raised seven children: Larry, Leroy, Treva, Verlinda, Carol, Eleanor, and Claire.

When Rena was learning to weave, she would sit behind her mother to watch. She would count the warp strings for each design block, and with these visual instructions, she wove her first rug, a Two Grey Hills style, all on her own. She sold it for 20 dollars. Much later in her career, she reminisces, she wove a very large Two Grey Hills rug and traded it for a red GMC truck at Rico Motors in Gallup!

For a time, Rena did not weave because of an illness; after she recovered, she took her place in what had become a family of artists. Her two sons, Leroy and Larry, learned silversmithing from their brother-in-law, Victor Beck, a well-known Navajo jeweler, and they would all show their work at top art shows—the Heard Museum's Indian Fair and Art

RENA BEGAY BEGAN WEAVING AT AGE SEVENTEEN TO AVOID AN ARRANGED MARRIAGE. THE MARRIAGE EVENTUALLY CAME TO PASS, AND SHE IS STILL WEAVING.

ABOVE: MODERN ART INFLUENCES CAN BE SEEN IN RENA'S TRADITIONAL RUGS, AND ON HER WALLS. ABOVE RIGHT: JUST A FEW OF THE AWARD RIBBONS RENA HAS RECEIVED FOR HER WORK.

Market in Phoenix and the Santa Fe Indian Market. They would collaborate on color combinations and designs. While attending these art shows, she was inspired by the work of other weavers to venture into weaving period pieces, particularly chief blankets from the 1800s. Her earlier work included Eye Dazzlers, Crystal, Ganado Red, and Two Grey Hills styles, which her mother, Marie Bekay, and her aunt, Lola Bekay, also wove.

Rena pushes the boundaries of the chief blanket and other period styles, along with the traditional styles she mastered earlier in her career, by using vivid color schemes and introducing modern design elements. She is considered to be a master weaver in the Classic Revival category.

When we visited Rena's home, she pulled out a big box of ribbons she has won in more than fifty-five years of weaving. As other visitors gasped, my sister Barbara and I were not surprised at all. Her weaving accolades have been consistent, and her rugs are in much demand by collectors who value not only the designs but also the high quality of her handspun, hand-dyed yarns.

Rena continues to weave one large rug for each art show she enters, plus several smaller rugs. Her physical limitations prevent her from processing her own materials these days, as the plant gathering and dye preparation are heavy work.

In addition to the awards and recognition she has gathered over the years, Rena's rugs are displayed in several public spaces, including one very large rug on permanent display at City Hall in Phoenix.

MARTHA GORMAN SCHULTZ

LEUPP, ARIZONA

BORN TO THE WATER'S EDGE CLAN, *Tábąąhá*

BORN FOR THE BITTER WATER CLAN, *Tódích'íi'nii*

Martha was born during the Great Depression. She remembers a lot about how her family lived during the Depression and the Navajo Livestock Reduction (see page 55), and later during the attack on Pearl Harbor and World War II, all of which had a great impact on her family. Martha remembers the rations available during the war when flour, coffee, sugar, salt, and raisins were in short supply. Her family ground dried corn into flour when there was no wheat flour to make bread. When the sugar was gone, they put hard candy into the coffee to melt.

As a child, Martha herded sheep and looked forward to attending school at Leupp Boarding School. The school was closed in 1942, though, when President Roosevelt signed an order to relocate and detain Japanese Americans in various relocation centers and isolation camps around the country. More than 120,000 Japanese Americans were sent to areas in the southwest. Leupp, Arizona, was the location picked for "problem inmates," with offenses such as demonstrating and protesting. One such crime consisted of calling a Caucasian nurse an "old maid." The Leupp isolation camp detained eighty men from April 1943 to when the camp was closed the following November. According to Martha, this interrupted her education; she says the United States government still owes her an education as promised in the Navajo Treaty of 1868.

Martha learned how to weave from her mother, Mary Gorman Clay, when she was eight years old. She wove a 30-by-30-inch single saddle blanket and sold it to the Leupp Trading Post for 2 dollars. A double saddle blanket measuring 30 inches by 60 inches would have been worth 4 dollars. As years went by, Martha mastered traditional styles such as Crystal, Wide Ruins, Two Grey Hills, and her specialty—Storm Pattern. Throughout her childhood, she continued to herd her family's flock of sheep, doing seasonal moves to different sheep camps. Sometimes she would camp at Canyon Diablo with her sister Helen. They used mules and donkeys to herd the sheep.

Martha and her husband raised twelve children: Sue, Marilou, Lola, Loretta, Jacob, Lena, Gloria, Virgil, Nona, Lula, Lavern, and Gary. Martha used to have a large flock of her own Churro sheep, but when her children were teenagers, she sold the lambs to buy their school clothes.

Martha is a master weaver, and in her healthier years, she processed all her own weaving materials, shearing, carding, spinning, and dyeing her wool. Martha taught her daughters how to weave, and she has incredibly talented weavers in her family. Her daughters, Marilou Schultz and Lola Cody, and her granddaughter, Melissa Cody, are premier weavers, garnering prestigious awards. Lola has won Best of Show at Santa Fe Indian Market for a very large Two Grey Hills rug. Martha shares a booth with her daughter Marilou at the Heard Museum's Indian Fair and Art Market in Phoenix, and at Santa Fe Indian Market. She has won many awards from these two art markets in addition to other art shows.

At age eighty-six, Martha spends many of her days in Flag-

OPPOSITE: MARTHA AND HER DAUGHTER LORETTA ENJOY A CRISP FALL DAY WITH A VIEW TO THE HILLS EAST OF FLAGSTAFF. LORETTA IS COLOR-BLIND, AND DEPENDS ON HER MOTHER AND DAUGHTER TO HELP WITH COLOR CHOICES.

staff with her daughter Loretta. Together they enjoy watching their favorite sports teams play on television. Because she still has her driver's license, Martha drives Loretta to work each day. Martha's physical health is impaired so she no longer has sheep. But like her mother, who was still weaving at the age of one hundred, she continues to weave.

LIVESTOCK REDUCTION

THE NAVAJO LIVESTOCK REDUCTION program carried out by the U.S. government in the 1930s began as a moderate idea to reduce the number of goats on the Navajo reservation. But as drought and damaging crop cultivation practices began to result in the infamous Dust Bowl years throughout the central and Midwest states, government agent John Collier began to take a closer look at the livestock population throughout the land of the Diné.

His estimation was that 500,000 sheep was the appropriate number for the more than 17 million acres of land. There were more than 2 million sheep, or about 9 sheep per acre. The edict was to reduce the number by half.

And so began a program of removal and slaughter that devastated the tribe financially, culturally, and emotionally. Women, who were the owners of the sheep in this matriarchal society, were not consulted or considered, and for many it was their only source of income. The pain lives on today.

LILLIE THOMAS TAYLOR

INDIAN WELLS, ARIZONA

BORN OF THE TOWERING HOUSE CLAN, *Kinyaa'áanii*

Lillie and her husband, Carl Taylor, a Navajo medicine man, raised nine children in Indian Wells: Dennis, Bernice, Herbert, Anita, Leonard, Rosie, Robert, Terry, and Diane. All eleven family members are artists in various media—jewelry, skilled crafts and trades, and weaving. Lillie, a fifth-generation Navajo master weaver, began weaving at an early age, between five and seven. She sold her first weaving, a saddle blanket, to the Indian Wells Trading Post; later she sold to the Leupp, Dilkon, and Bidahochee Trading Posts. Lillie's mother would draw the designs for her and for her older sister, Lucy.

Lillie was born during the Great Depression, and her childhood was marked by one hardship after another. While the "Indian New Deal," or Indian Reorganization Act of 1934, worked well at promoting faster economic recovery for some tribes, it was especially ineffective for the Navajo. It included the disastrous Livestock Reduction (page 55), which devastated her family and many others. Then World War II caused the closing of the Leupp Boarding School, which Lillie and her sister attended. It was converted into a Japanese internment camp, leaving many Navajo children without the means to gain an education. These are painful memories, even today. Yet all these challenges made Lillie into who she is today—a very strong, traditional Diné woman who has raised a large family, with each child going on to become a

LILLIE HAS BEEN A PROLIFIC WEAVER, ALWAYS TRYING NEW STYLES. HARDSHIPS THROUGHOUT HER LIFE HAVE MADE HER THE TOUGH WOMAN SHE IS TODAY.

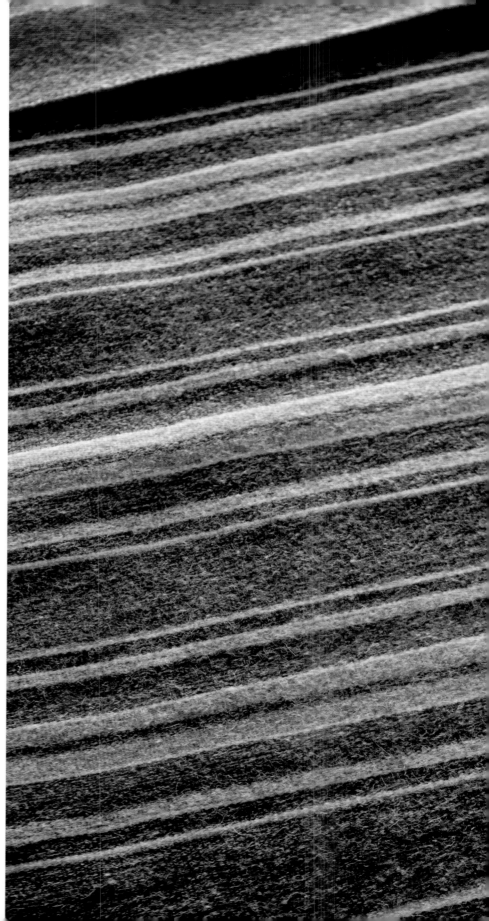

THE SUBTLE NATURAL HUES OF SOME OF LILLIE'S RUGS ECHO
THE STRATA OF SURROUNDING MESAS.

productive, hardworking adult. She lives in a house she built in 2004 with money from her weaving. It is on the site that was once the family's winter sheep camp.

As most elders who lived through the Depression, Lillie never wastes anything—she even saves little bits of leftover wool to be recarded or respun. In her earlier years, she harvested plants for dyeing and was known to explore and experiment, always going beyond the predictable or the common notion that one plant has only one use. One of her favorite dyes comes from the bark of juniper roots, which gives a warm reddish pink. The root is also useful for sweeping up dust devils, and spanking the kids, she says.

A devastating loss occurred in August 1996, when Lillie was sixty-five. Her son, famed Navajo jeweler Herbert Taylor, the son who used a lot of her rug designs in his highly collectible jewelry, a trendsetter who eagerly introduced her to many of his collectors, the son with whom she shared booths at art shows and who motivated his artistic family to higher standards, passed on. The surviving family was plunged into the darkest recesses of human grief.

But grief can shape one in a variety of ways. Lillie and Carl had raised a strong family with traditional teachings, prayers, songs, and beautiful ceremonies. Honoring these traditions cracked open the dark recesses to let in light, and healing began for the family. Lillie found solace in her preparations for weaving; she experimented with carding Merino and Churro wools and adding in mohair, which gives her yarn a special luster. Lillie laughingly says that she wore out many wool carders with these experiments.

With sheer determination and pluck, Lillie revitalized her weaving style, developing a fine thread count with vibrant colors that she applies to her Ganado Red, Eye Dazzler, and Wide Ruins patterns; to her chief blankets, pictorials, rug dresses, and sand paintings; and to her Two Grey Hills, Teec Nos Pos, Storm Pattern, and Yei rugs. Her business card tagline says, "Weaving her dream," a very appropriate self-de-

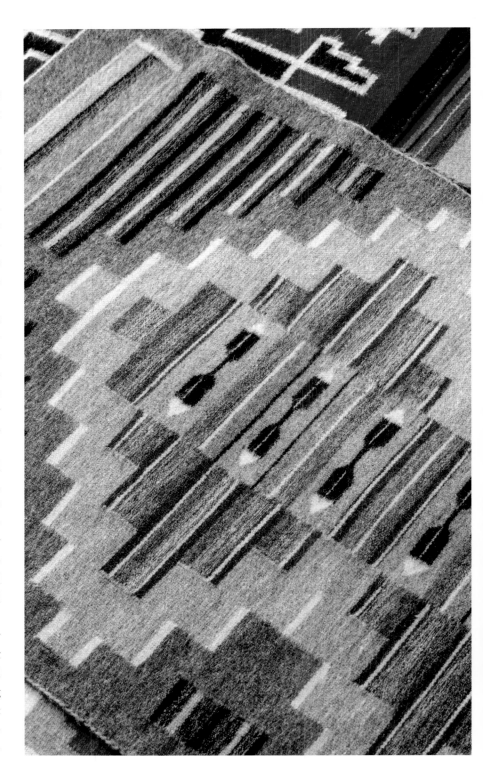

scription. I asked Lillie if there is a style she hasn't woven, and she replied, "I worked my whole life, I put every bit of energy I have into everything I do. I am very busy, I have no time for gossip." Hearing this, Barbara and I did fist pumps! We admire her greatly.

These days, Lillie sells her rugs at the Heard Museum's Indian Fair and Art Market in Phoenix, and at the Santa Fe Indian Market. She has garnered many weaving awards and was celebrated as one of Arizona's Living Treasures in 2000.

DIANE TAYLOR BEALL

BORN OF THE TOWERING HOUSE CLAN, *Kinyaa'áanii*

Diane is the baby of the Taylor family, having eight older brothers and sisters. At the start of her own artistic life, Diane started to learn jewelry making until she had a mishap with her long hair caught in the buffing machine. Diane learned how to weave from her mother, Lillie.

She accompanied her mother to sell her rugs at the local trading posts, but even at a young age, she noticed the discrepancy in the prices on rug tags and the price that was given to the weavers. "This is not right; we have to take out the middleman," she thought. She knew her mother worked hard to make quality rugs; she processed all her materials, harvested plants for bright or muted colors, and she learned diverse weaving styles all on her own. Diane watched her mother experiment with weaving and dyeing. They spent a lot of time at their sheep corral. In fact, Diane refers to the useful knowledge she acquired from those days as "lessons from the corral."

Around 1985, Diane asked her mother what she would think if she decided to run for Miss Navajo, a highly competitive contest for the high honor of representing the Navajo people. It requires a year's commitment, and the judging criteria are very tough. Instead of hearing her mother say to her, "Yes, you should run," her mother asked her, "Are you ready?" which in essence was more of a challenge. Are you ready to put your lessons of the family's teachings, the spo-

DIANNE TAYLOR BEALL, A FORMER MISS NAVAJO NATION, VALUES HER TRAINING AS A WEAVER AS WELL AS HER UNIVERSITY DEGREE IN COMMUNITY DEVELOPMENT.

ken Navajo language, preparation of Navajo foods, sheep butchering, and mastery of the Navajo arts into achieving this position? Diane accepted the challenge and in her talent competition, she sang the sacred spindle song in Navajo while holding her Navajo lap spindle. Diane reigned as Miss Navajo from 1986 to 1987.

Diane finished a master's degree in community development from the University of New Mexico in Santa Fe in December of 2017. At four years old, in the sheep corral, she decided she wanted to have a master's degree. When she received her acceptance letter to the master's program at UNM, she went out to the sheep corral to open it up. She tells her mom "Thank you for raising me in a corral."

It is finished in beauty.

SPIDER WOMAN'S SONS

IN OUR NAVAJO universe, we are in balance when we accept our family and kinship roles, and these roles emulate the forces of nature in our universe. The forces can exhibit male energy or female energy. We need male and female energies to create harmony and to immerse ourselves in the beauty of these energies. Everywhere you look, in printed media, in visual media, Navajo women are portrayed to be in the primary roles of weavers in their families. But there have always been male weavers. Of the male weavers we present here, none have children. But most are or have been in caretaker roles.

Navajo gender roles are blurred, because we were once a very strong matriarchal society. There is a Navajo phrase that was a cultural rule to live by before Bosque Redondo and the Long Walk: Self-Reliance, *Táá hó'ájit'éégóó*. Self-reliance does not define gender roles, who takes care of whom, who does the cooking, cleaning, taking care of children; it is dependent on which family member is available, whether male or female.

Of course, after the Long Walk ended in the 1870s, the Navajo people weren't able to be self-reliant anymore. They were forced to be dependent on the government. All the historical trauma that sprang from that is still going on today. At the same time, our cultural values have held firm. Today, men might become weavers to carry on family tradition, to give assistance to their aging mothers and grandmothers who weave, or to mentor the next generation. While their numbers are fewer, male weavers achieve the same excellence in their work as their female counterparts, as you will see in the following stories.

GILBERT NEZ BEGAY

CROWNPOINT, NEW MEXICO

BORN OF THE MEXICAN CLAN, *Naakaii Dine'é*

BORN FOR THE RED-RUNNING-INTO-THE-WATER CLAN,
Táchii'nii

MOTHER'S FATHER, TOWERING HOUSE PEOPLE,
Kinyaa'áanii

FATHER'S FATHER, WATER'S EDGE CLAN, *Tábąąhá*

Gilbert's mother, Gladys C. Thompson, raised him in Mari-ano Lake, New Mexico, but Gilbert spent part of his childhood with the paternal side of his family in the Red Valley area of the Navajo Nation, just north of Shiprock, New Mexico, at the base of Arizona's Carrizo Mountains. Gilbert's paternal grandmother, Tsé'tah Bistie's front door faced the iconic, volcanic Shiprock rock formation named *Tsé Bit'a'í*, winged rock. His grandmother was a weaver. She wove Two Grey Hills and Teec Nos Pos styles, and a distinc-tive style of Yei rugs with white backgrounds. Navajo textile scholar, Ron Garnanez, who is the current president of Sheep is Life (see page 96) says that she helped Despah Tutt Nez, a renowned Red Rock sand painting textile weaver, to develop certain sand painting figures to be woven into rugs as well. Gilbert's paternal grandmother's brother was Tsé tah Begay, a well-known medicine man who has recorded corn grinding songs that are still being played on the area's radio stations.

**IN ADDITION TO HIS WEAVING EXPERTISE, GILBERT IS A
MASTER JEWELRY MAKER. HERE HE IS WEARING SOME OF
HIS WORK.**

Gilbert herded sheep with his grandmother in the open range near the Shiprock pinnacle. She would take her small spindle and spin wool as they watched the herd graze, and she would regale Gilbert with stories. Here's one that exemplifies Navajo humor and reticence: One day a friend came over to visit from Mitten Rock, located between White Rock and Red Rock Valley. Gilbert's grandmother was carding black wool and placing the rolags on her left side where the woman sat. As his grandmother turned to her right side to get more wool to be placed on her handcarders, the sneaky friend tucked some rolags inside her big silver concho belt. His grandmother noticed but did not react in action or in words. She continued to card more wool while the woman fidgeted. When the visit was over and the woman was walking away, his grandmother noticed a piece of black rolag hanging out from her tsiiyééł—now an extremely extra-large Navajo hair bun, much bigger than when she first arrived! (In his grandmother's time, true black-colored wool was hard to get from sheep, and the trading posts did not have black dye packets available.)

Another story she loved to tell was about the "pound rug" days from about 1900 to the 1930s, when traders bought rugs from weavers by the pound. With a twinkle in her eye, she said they outsmarted the traders by sprinkling fine dirt into their rugs to have them weigh more. Ultimately, the traders caught on and asked for cleaner rugs to be brought in.

Gilbert's maternal grandmother, Julie C. Thompson, was from Mariano Lake. She wove Gallup throws and Crystal styles of rugs. Gilbert learned how to weave from his maternal grandmother when he was eleven years old and in the fourth grade. His grandmother often corrected his weaving errors, and Gilbert listened, watched, and learned everything she taught. From these grandmothers, he became fully immersed in historical weaving legacy stories of both sides of his family. He cherishes his grandmother's spinning and weaving tools: an oak batten that he had repaired, another dark one with grooves from use, and others.

Gilbert has lived in Crownpoint, New Mexico, since 1988;

GILBERT TREASURES AND USES HIS GRANDMOTHER'S WEAVING TOOLS.

GILBERT, AN AVID BRONCOS FOOTBALL FAN (NOTE THE LICENSE PLATE) STOPPED ON HIS WAY TO WORK IN FARMINGTON TO SHOW US HIS PRIZE-WINNING TWO-FACED WEAVING. THIS STYLE OF WEAVING IS RARE AND REQUIRES SPECIAL SKILLS.

he commutes more than eighty miles one way to Farmington, New Mexico, where he works at Safeway as a general merchandise manager. He is a part-time but very productive weaver. He weaves about two inches per day on a rug. He can weave a small rug in two weeks if he works continuously; he likes to weave outdoors as much as possible. Weaving fine projects can take him up to three months, but he gets bored and ends up starting other projects. It takes him three to four years to spin enough yarn to weave a six-foot-long rug, using wool from the Navajo Sheep Project (see page 96).

Gilbert's rugs are multiple twills, diamonds, and weft-faced double weave—rugs that have completely different patterns on each side. Gilbert's mother took him to a neighbor in Mariano Lake to learn the two-face weaving, and her condition was for Gilbert not to teach other weavers her self-taught, rare technique. She gave him one verbal lesson and Gilbert had to do fancy math to get the counts of the different patterns of twill to come out even on both sides. He makes up designs as he weaves, not planning them out in advance. He has his own pattern, which is a combination of both of his grandmothers' patterns.

More than rugs, though, Gilbert also weaves rug dresses, rug vests, horse cinches, handbags, sash belts, and other functional apparel. He often includes the traditional four lines in the rug dresses, in symbolic hope that women always have four directions to escape. He weaves some dresses with black wool, a tradition that began so that women wouldn't be seen as they tried to escape the conquistadors at night.

Gilbert shows and sells his weavings annually at the Heard Museum's Indian Fair and Art Market in Phoenix and at

FITTING HIS WEAVING TIME IN BETWEEN A FULL-TIME JOB AND THREE HOURS OF COMMUTING EACH DAY, GILBERT IS REMARKABLY PRODUCTIVE. THESE RUGS ARE HANDSPUN, NATURAL-COLORED WOOL.

RUG DRESSES ARE WOVEN FOR SPECIAL OCCASIONS, SUCH AS SCHOOL GRADUATIONS. EACH ONE IS DESIGNED TO REFLECT THE CHARACTER AND PERSONALITY OF ITS WEARER.

the Santa Fe Indian Market. Both are prestigious Indian art markets and are juried shows. He also has developed a group of fans on social media who are eager to buy his woven handbags and horse cinches. Gilbert's work has been in several weaving exhibitions, including *Weaving in the Margins: Navajo Men as Weavers* at the Museum of Indian Arts and Culture in Santa Fe, and *Diné Dah' Atl'ó, Men Who Weave: A Revival in Dine Bikeyah* at the Navajo Nation Museum in Window Rock. His work also appeared in an exhibition of contemporary weavings by young Dine artists, *Gifts from Spider Woman's Grandchildren*, at the Amerind Foundation and Museum in Dragoon, Arizona.

NATHAN HARRY

RED ROCK, RED ROCK VALLEY, NEW MEXICO

BORN OF THE RED-RUNNING-INTO-THE-WATER CLAN, *Táchii'nii*

BORN FOR THE COYOTE PASS PEOPLE, *Mą'ii Deeshgiizhinii*

MOTHER'S FATHER, MEXICAN PEOPLE CLAN, *Naakaii Dine'é*

FATHER'S FATHER, WATER'S EDGE PEOPLE, *Tábąąhá*

Nathan is in his mid-thirties and a cousin to Gilbert Begay. Nathan was born and raised along with four siblings in the Red Rock Valley area in New Mexico, very close to the Tsé Bit a í, the iconic Shiprock rock formation. Nathan watched his grandmother, Nellie Harry, and his mother, Marilyn Yazzie, weave. As a young child, he helped with the process of sheep shearing, cleaning wool, spinning, and other tasks of Navajo weaving. While attending Shiprock High School, he became intrigued by an Anglo schoolteacher doing a Navajo arts and crafts demonstration on pottery, basketry, and weaving. He particularly was fascinated by how the teacher took a box, sawed little perforations on each end, and put warp strings on it. Nathan laughed to himself as he pictured his grandmother's and mother's intricate way of warping and setting up their looms compared to the teacher's simple paper box loom.

With his interest now fully piqued, he went home and set up his first rug with help from his grandmother. It was an easy learning experience because he had been immersed in weaving tasks at a young age; it was already in his artistic system. His grandmother was delighted; she had woven all her life and he believes that she wanted the family tradition to continue through him.

His grandmother bought his first rug for 10 dollars to encourage him to keep weaving. His siblings have left home to pursue education or employment, but Nathan is concerned about his aging grandmother and has chosen to stay home to take care of her. He has been a full-time weaver since he was nineteen.

Nathan weaves a lot of different styles: Tree of Life, pictorials depicting modern life, landscapes, Classic Revival styles of Third Phase Chief Blankets, contemporary Moqui style, Teec Nos Pos, Ganado, rug dresses, Two Grey Hills, and Nathan's favorite, the Storm Pattern. Nathan has strong creative design skills, but he is careful to stick to "trading post styles" because that is what sells. But one day he would like to stop doing those styles and weave what interests him. "Weaving is something that I do from deep down in my soul. I'm a Navajo and Navajos are known for weaving, so it's something that I can be proud of," Nathan said. "Some think that because I am young, I am just playing around with it. But I know that deep down in my heart I do this for me and for my people and to keep our traditions going and keep our heritage alive."

Nathan sells his work to Foutz Trading Post in Shiprock, Notah-Dineh Trading Company and Museum in Cortez, Colorado, and Toh-Atin Gallery in Durango, Colorado. Nathan participates regularly with the Friends of Hubbell Native American Arts Auction put on by Burnham Trading Post. He has sold to Garland's Navajo Rugs in Sedona, Arizona.

NATHAN'S RUG CONTAINS GEOMETRIC PATTERNS AND LIGHT-NING-LIKE ZIGZAGS OF HIS FAVORITE STYLE, THE STORM PATTERN.

Nathan said he is limited by his ability to travel further to sell his work; it is time consuming and daunting when he needs a navigator to find addresses. Nathan has an annual booth at the Heard Museum Indian Fair and Art Market in Phoenix, and he does regional demonstrations upon request. Nathan's work has been in two exhibitions: the Navajo Nation Museum exhibition *Diné Dah' Atl'ó, Men Who Weave: A Revival in Dine Bikeyah,* and the Amerind Foundation and Museum's exhibit in Dragoon, Arizona of contemporary weavings by young Diné artists entitled, *Gifts from Spider Woman's Grandchildren.*

NELLIE HARRY

BORN OF THE RED-RUNNING-INTO-THE-WATER CLAN, *Táchii'nii*

BORN FOR THE WATER'S EDGE PEOPLE, *Tábąąhá*

MOTHER'S GRANDFATHER, RED HOUSE PEOPLE, *Kinłichíi'nii*

FATHER'S GRANDFATHER, YUCCA FRUIT-STRUNG-OUT-IN-A-LINE CLAN, *Hashk'ąą Hadzohí*

Nathan's grandmother, Nellie Harry, might be eighty-five years old, but doesn't know for sure. She was born in the late 1920s, she thinks, into a family of twelve children. Her sisters all were weavers, and her brothers helped by carding and spinning the wool. One of her brothers had a herd of white Churros. Where she and Nathan live now was their family's winter camp. They took the sheep to the mountains during the summer.

Nellie still weaves, though she needs Nathan to warp her loom. Nellie has woven a lot of Yei rugs: the figures with square heads were women, and round heads were men. In days gone by, she sold her rugs to the nearest trading post for half cash and half supplies. But that trading post is now more of a convenience store and doesn't buy rugs.

Nellie remembers the Livestock Reduction clearly, which began in 1934 and lasted through the late 1940s. The horrific way that her family's livestock was slaughtered has stayed with her.

As an adult, she cultivated her own flock of sheep, goats, and horses. On the day we visited Nathan and Nellie, we saw a herd of magnificent horses; later we learned they were hers and that she continues to ride them to follow her sheep. In November 2017, there was a horse roundup by the Navajo Nation's Agriculture Department to control the feral horses that are depleting natural resources and threatening the population of the domesticated livestock. However well-intentioned the tribe's efforts have been to solve this problem, the sheer number of 40,000 wild horses that roam the Nation's lands prevents the tribe's agents from always checking to see which horses are feral and which belong to someone. They rounded up Nellie's horses and now there are only four remaining. Another injustice visited on a strong Navajo woman who has stood the test of time to rebuild after these tragic events.

CLOCKWISE FROM RIGHT: SHIPROCK, AN ICONIC GEOLOGICAL OUTCROPPING, LOOMS BEHIND NELLIE AT HER FAMILY HOME IN RED ROCK VALLEY.

ONLY FOUR OF NELLIE'S LARGE HERD OF HORSES REMAIN AFTER A RESERVATION-WIDE CULLING OF FERAL HORSES.

EVEN LEFTOVER BITS OF YARN HAVE USE AND VALUE.

JASON HARVEY

SANOSTEE, NEW MEXICO

BORN OF THE SALT WATER CLAN, *Todik'ozhi*

BORN FOR THE RED BOTTOM PEOPLE, *Tł'ááshchí'í*

When Jason Harvey was young, he would watch his grandmother and mother weaving. He listened to the beats of their weaving combs. The cadence of the beats sounded like heartbeats and he knew he wanted to learn how to weave. His family of weavers is known for their Storm Pattern rugs. Jason finally learned to weave at age sixteen and wove a Two Grey Hills style that he chose to keep and did not sell.

Jason attended college in Farmington, New Mexico, and took care of his elderly grandparents. After his grandparents passed away, he took a part-time job as a visiting caretaker for Navajo elders. He loved the work and supplemented his income with his part-time weaving.

At his homestead in tiny, remote Sanostee, New Mexico, at the foot of the Chuska Mountains, his family raises sheep, chickens, and turkeys. His family is also known for plant dyeing, using rock lichen (for orange), ground lichen, juniper berries (for shades of gray and blue), sheep manure (for beige), coffee grounds, onion skins, sage, indigo, dock roots, wild carrots (for yellow), Navajo tea, and cochineal. Along with vegetal dyes, Jason supplements his stash of wool with processed and dyed commercial yarn, bought at Burnham Trading Post in Sanders, Arizona. Seventeen years after learning to weave, Jason is now teaching his aunts while weaving full-time himself. He is a soft-spoken gentleman but

JASON'S VIBRANT STORM PATTERN RUG STANDS IN CONTRAST TO THE SOFTER NATURAL DYES HE OFTEN USES.

successfully sells weavings that speak loudly and boldly of his talents. His styles include Yei and Germantown—revivals of old-time styles of the late 1800s—and Storm Pattern rugs, all combined with an extensive palette of vegetal-dyed hues. He also likes weaving "sampler" rugs, in which different motifs are inset like rugs within rugs. Jason can make complicated sampler designs mixed with the old trading post styles but prefers to keep these designs relatively simple so as not to tax the brains so much. But you may need to take a refresher course in geometry just to follow the diagonals within his geometric designs. He does not sketch out his designs, but lets his available wool colors drive his creative force. The results are stunning in design and in color combinations, and his weavings are now unmistakable because he weaves in a "signature," a backward letter J.

Jason has participated in various shows and exhibits such as the Navajo Nation Museum's male weavers exhibit in Window Rock, Arizona, and *Gifts from Spiderwoman's Grandhildren* at the Amerind Foundation and Museum in Dragoon, Arizona. As his weaving techniques improved, he was juried into the Heard Museum's annual Indian Art Fair and Market in Phoenix, and the Santa Fe Indian Market. Jason also secured a fellowship with the Southwestern Association of Indian Arts (SWAIA) in in 2000. SWAIA is the nonprofit organization that puts on the prestigious Santa Fe Indian Market every year in August. These fellowships are offered each year and the competition is fierce.

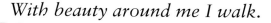

With beauty around me I walk.

WEAVERS IN THE HEART OF LIFE

FOR GENERATIONS, NAVAJO weaving has stood true and tough through social, economic, and culture shifts on and off the Navajo Nation. History has not been kind. Presidential executive orders have terminated and banished many of us from our precious homeland, beyond the protection of our four sacred mountains. Economic hardships created politically or otherwise, the loss of cultural knowledge, and negative movements to terminate our language, culture, and livelihood have only given us a deeper motivation to survive.

We are the enduring Diné. We have persevered through warfare, starvation, and forced relocations. We are warriors. Most of us are given warrior names at birth; our umbilical cords are buried on our homesteads. We honor these warrior names by living each day, rising with the sun, giving our blessings, and being productive to the best of our potential, to be in Hózhó. Hózhó is our way of life, to live in balance and beauty. We do not separate the weaving arts from our culture, spirituality, daily life, or our connection to the earth. Weaving is a way for us to live in balance.

We strive for the four values of life:
· The value we hold for life itself
· Our work—for us, it is weaving
· Our family, extended family, friends, and communal relationships
· Our view of developing, acquiring, and passing on knowledge
When we live these ideals, we are well balanced.

The weavers you will meet in this chapter exemplify these values. They have known hard times, but they have persevered to achieve excellence in their craft. As firmly established weavers, their strength anchors their families as they are able to care for elders and nourish the young. They know the value of looking behind and looking ahead. They walk in Hózhó.

FLORENCE MANYGOATS

WHITE MESA AREA OF TONALEA, ARIZONA

BORN OF THE BITTER WATER CLAN, *Tódích'íi'nii*

BORN FOR THE RED HOUSE CLAN, *Kinłichii'nii*

MOTHER'S FATHER, TANGLE PEOPLE, *Ta'neeszahnii*

FATHER'S FATHER, MEXICAN PEOPLE CLAN, *Naakaii Dine'é*

Florence was born in 1959 to Bill and Lula Scott in the White Mesa area of Tonalea, Arizona. Florence has three sisters; none weave. Her children are Jayson, Clayton, Jarrett, Vanessa, B. J., and Conray, all adults now. Two were adopted. None weave.

Florence learned to weave from her mother when she was about eight and finished her first rug when she was nine. She sold it to a trading post for 5 dollars and a bag of candy. Her mother took care of their flock of sheep and gathered plants for dyeing around Jacob Lake, near the edge of the Grand Canyon. Her specialty of weaving was the Storm Pattern. Florence's grandmother was also a weaver and wove saddle blankets. For many years, the family participated in shearing the sheep and cleaning and skirting the wool. Florence's mother gathered plants and dyed the wool; her aunts carded the wool and Florence and her sister spun the wool.

Florence was in the Indian Student Placement Program run by the Mormon Church when she was young, from the second grade to the fifth grade. This program allowed Mormon families to enter the reservation and take foster children to be educated in white schools.

THE STRIKING COLORS IN FLORENCE'S RUGS ACCENTUATE THE COLORS OF HER LANDSCAPE.

She returned to her family during her junior high school years and later attended Tuba City High School, where she took a refresher course in Navajo weaving in the arts and crafts class. During the summers, she wove, and with the sales, she bought her school clothes.

Florence's first husband was Clark Yazzie of the Yazzie weaving family, specifically the family of famed weaver Larry Yazzie, her husband's brother. Larry Yazzie developed his own style of weaving, which is known as the Blue Canyon style, and her mother-in-law taught her the Raised Outline style. Being in the Yazzie family for fifteen years

gave her the skills to develop her own style of weaving, which combines the Raised Outline and the Blue Canyon styles.

In her time of raising six children, Florence wove to provide for her family. At times she would take her rugs to the trading post, and early on, she became very attuned to the criticisms she received. The traders would deduct money for crooked edges, uneven designs, and various other errors. One trader told her, "If you consider yourself a professional weaver, you should bring rugs woven by a professional weaver." She would go home and consider the criticisms, noting what she could do to earn the highest possible price. She often would think of what her mother would say to her: "If you have a work in progress, your mind should be there, not elsewhere."

Eventually, Florence looked beyond the trading post to sell her rugs. In 2000, she entered the Heard Museum's Indian Fair and Art Market in Phoenix, and the Santa Fe Indian Market, and was finally able to sell directly to collectors and set firm prices for her large three-by-six-foot rugs.

In 2002, with all her adult children living away from home, Florence received a phone call from Los Angeles—a grandbaby was about to be born. The father was one of her sons. Florence called her sister to relay the glad tidings and as family members received the news, they all drove their vehicles and caravanned to Los Angeles to wait for the birth of her grandson, Juelz. Such is the Navajo way. Florence returned home with her grandson to Tonalea and entered a new phase of life. Weaving was put on the back burner.

As her grandson grew, Florence went back to her weaving, but this time she started mixing commercial wool in with her vegetal-dyed wool to create her masterpieces because her time was limited and the hard work of spinning and dyeing was getting too physically challenging for her. She has a disciplined weaving schedule around Juelz's school activities. On a full day of weaving, she will weave in the morning, take an hour for lunch while she watches an episode of *Law and Order* on television, and once it is over, she's back to the loom.

These days, she no longer views her weaving as a chore, a struggle to provide for her family. Her husband, Leland Manygoats, works in construction in other cities and states. Florence will pick a new art show to enter her rugs and upon acceptance, she plans a vacation around the show. She and her grandson will drive to the city, stopping for sightseeing, and Leland will fly in from wherever he is working. They will attend the art show and then enjoy the city, pick an activity, discover new places to eat, and enjoy the family time. She now considers her weaving more of a serious hobby than a necessity.

Not long ago, my family and I were at an art show and I was walking around for a little break when I saw Florence and her grandson at her booth. I watched Juelz teasing her, and then as people walked up, he sat back, watched, and listened as his grandmother talked about her rugs for sale. When they asked for photos, Juelz politely backed out of view. Once the customers were gone, he and Florence went right back to their conversation, laughing, Florence with an adoring smile for her grandson.

Before anyone laments that none of her children have picked up the art of weaving, know that her grandson will continue her legacy through her weaving stories. He can pick out a photo of her rug and tell stories of its being on the loom, where it was sold, what they did on their trips with that rug. His woven stories will delight his children and grandchildren, and maybe inspire one to take up the art.

RABBITBRUSH YIELDS SHADES OF YELLOW AND GOLD.

ROSALITA TELLER

CHINLE, ARIZONA

BORN OF THE DEER SPRING CLAN, *Bįįh bitoodnii*

BORN FOR THE WATER FLOWS TOGETHER CLAN, *Tó'aheedlíinii*

MOTHER'S FATHER, TOWERING HOUSE CLAN, *Kinyaa'áanii*

FATHER'S FATHER, BITTER WATER CLAN, *Tódích'íi'nii*

Rosalita was born in 1975 to Louise and Kee B. Tsosie. She and her four siblings grew up living in Canyon de Chelly, Arizona, in the summer and in Chinle during the winter because their access to water in the canyon was limited and the trucked-in water would freeze. She helped her family farm during the summer in their broad swath of land cradled by steep ochre walls of canyon stone. They called their land *Tsé ya linii* (hole in the rock) because of the enormous hole in the canyon wall at the western edge of their property. They grew corn, melons, and squash, and they had a plum orchard.

Rosalita learned to weave when she was nine years old. She and her mother acquired their wool from relatives in the canyon who had sheep. They would clean, card, spin, and dye with plants harvested in the canyon. Rosalita's style of weaving is mainly the Chinle style, with distinctive design elements known as Chinle stars and Chinle squash blossoms. She uses her vegetal-dyed wool for the most part, but lately, she has begun mixing it with commercial wool.

She is a *Yei bi cheii* dancer and has learned all about the traditional ceremonies from her father—he really pushed tradition on the children in her family, which she's glad about now. The Navajos who do the yei bi cheii ceremonies are taught strict rules of conduct. If they are also weavers, only they can weave that style of rug; otherwise, it can bring harm to other weavers.

Rosalita and Rodger Teller were married in 1994 and are

ROSALITA TREASURES TIME SPENT ON FAMILY LAND IN CANYON DE CHELLY. HERE SHE IS WORKING ON A RUG IN THE "HAIR BUN" MOTIF.

AILLA IS THIRTEEN YEARS OLD AND IS IN THE EIGHTH GRADE
AT CHINLE JUNIOR HIGH SCHOOL. SHE LIKES GOING TO
SCHOOL, AND HER SECOND-FAVORITE PASTIME IS READING A
LOT OF BOOKS. WHEN SHE HAS FREE TIME, SHE ENJOYS HER
MOST-FAVORITE PASTIME, WHICH IS WEAVING.

raising four children, Shawn-Codi, Crystal, Ailla, and Rodgina. Rosalita was working as a certified guide and driver for a jeep tour company when, tragically, her younger sister passed on, leaving six children, the youngest under a year of age. Rosalita and Rodger took in the children and she has had to put her guide and driving job on hold. Once the youngest starts school, Rosalita plans on getting her recertification. Meanwhile, she is weaving and making silver jewelry to supplement the family's income, sometimes selling to tourists in the canyon at a makeshift market near the Antelope Ruins petroglyphs.

LOUISE TSOSIE

CHINLE, ARIZONA

BORN OF THE DEER SPRING CLAN, *Bįįh Bitoodnii*

BORN FOR THE TOWERING HOUSE CLAN, *Kinyaa'áanii*

MOTHER'S FATHER, ZUNI CLAN, *Tachi'nii*

FATHER'S FATHER, WATER'S EDGE CLAN, *Tábąąhá*

LOUISE TSOSIE, ROSALITA'S MOTHER, LEARNED TO WEAVE FROM HER FATHER, SILARGO BEGAY.

Silargo Begay raised his daughter Louise, Rosalita's mother, in Low Mountain, Arizona, northeast of Flagstaff. When Louise was very young, her mother became ill and Silargo feared there would not be time for her to teach Louise all the things a Navajo mother should teach her child. So he had his wife teach him various traditional arts such as weaving, basket making, and making holistic herbal medicine. He learned how to process the wool, make weaving tools, warp a loom, and weave. When his wife passed, Silargo was ready to teach his daughter everything he had learned.

Louise learned the art of Navajo weaving, of creating Navajo baskets used for ceremonies, and of making herbal medicines. As Louise learned more and more from her father, she started weaving Third Phase Chief Blankets, Tree of Life, Germantown Revivals, Two Grey Hills, and Storm Pattern rugs. She still uses the weaving tools her father made for her.

Now Louise is a full-time weaver; weaving is her only source of income, so she is very industrious. When she has needed to sell quickly, amazingly, without a vehicle, she has hitchhiked from Chinle to Crownpoint, New Mexico, to enter her rugs in the monthly rug auction and returned home the same day. In a vehicle, it is a 264-mile round-trip. When I gasped, she said, "People these days spend too much time not walking. They go to the hospital and get on medication. When you weave sitting down, you need to walk, you have to be healthy to weave." She continued, "I go to the chapter house and run into people that are younger than me and they look sick and old. I get on the road at 7 a.m. and will only accept a ride with folks I know. I get to the auction, sell my rugs, get a ride home because by then, it's dark." Her daughter Rosalita says, "I used to tell my mom to wait for me, because I needed to get the kids to school or do other family errands. But she is impatient and will start walking to sell her rugs. I won't let her do that anymore—she is seventy-eight years old! I give her a ride." I look at Louise and she has the final words: "I need to sell my rugs."

KATHERINE PAYMELLA

CANYON DE CHELLY, ARIZONA

BORN OF THE TOWERING HOUSE CLAN, *Kinyaa'áanii*

Katherine Paymella's parents and grandparents lived in Canyon de Chelly. Her grandmother raised her there, and they followed the sheep through the seasons. They would run the sheep in the summer in the canyon for two months, then on the rim for one month, then in the mountains. Now Katherine is in the canyon year-round, living in a traditional hogan, but spending some time to commute to a house near Chinle where her husband lives. She has three children and several grandchildren.

Her grandmother taught her to weave and spin, and she weaves throughout the seasons. "Weaving is just about life," she says. "It teaches you a lot of patience." Katherine believes that your weaving will tell you stories if you let it. She never has a plan before she begins weaving, no ideas of design or color, but she has a vision of what the design will be. Katherine emphasizes the sacred aspects of weaving, saying it is not art or for money: "It has purpose for the family, for the world." The Story, she tells us, says that when there's a threat of war, weave all the time. With your design, you win the battle.

Katherine says you have to pay attention to your setting. When you weave, your mind is emptied. She cards, spins, and skeins, and then after skeining, she washes the yarn. She likes Chinle designs: the squiggly lines represent the waves of

KATHERINE PAYMELLA VIEWS WEAVING AS PLAYING A PART IN THE PURPOSE OF LIFE.

the water. (Chinle means "water coming out of the canyon.") Katherine also weaves rug dresses. Because they are so difficult to take on and off, she innovated a new design, weaving a separate skirt and blouse. When worn together, it has the appearance of a traditional rug dress.

Quality and attention to detail are important to her. When her granddaughter wove a small rug, Katherine asked her, "What is the rug telling you? This rug is laughing at you—see

OPPOSITE: MANY STYLES OF RUG USING HANDSPUN SHEEP'S WOOL FROM HER FLOCK AND VEGETAL DYES FROM HER LAND ORNAMENT KATHERINE'S HOGAN IN CANYON DE CHELLY.

LEFT: KATHERINE WALKS HER LAND DAILY, CHECKING ON SHEEP AND GOATS, ORCHARD TREES, CORN CROP.

BELOW: KATHERINE USES PLANTS FROM HER LAND TO CREATE A RANGE OF COLORS. HERE SHE PREPARES A SKEIN FOR THE DYEPOT.

the teeth?" She was referring to the vertical white lines of exposed warp—a sign that the weft hadn't been properly beaten in. This prompted the granddaughter to weave a second rug.

The farm where Katherine lives has been in her family for generations. She grows corn and has an orchard of apple, plum, cherry, and apricot trees. Her sheep and goat herds are corralled against walls of the canyon. After the Navajos returned from the Long Walk in 1868, each family was given ten trees. Katherine is replanting offshoots from some of the original Canyon peaches; they are sensitive and great care goes into tending them as saplings, but once they grow, they are the most hardy of all the fruit trees, and the ripe fruit is better tasting than the peaches from the stores.

Katherine does a lot of natural dyeing. She gets different shades from the same plant, depending on the season. She uses plum juice for purple (or brown if they ripen too long), prickly pear and sumac for red, wild carrot root for gold. Her favorite dye plant is walnut, which grows in the canyon, for the variety of browns it gives throughout the seasons. Katherine keeps gloves, boots, bags, and a shovel in her truck; when she drives to pick up her grandchildren or for a long-distance errand, she looks out for plants. She doesn't premordant her wool skeins, preferring to combine the dried plants and mordant in the same pot. Some of the wool skeins are briefly dipped, some are boiled longer, and she gets a muted but wide range of colors that complement each other in her rugs. She also watches the weather; she prefers clear, sunny days to dye. If there is even a brief cloud cover, it will affect her color pot.

She doesn't say, "dye," but "color." She asked her eight-year-old niece who was visiting if she thought it was a good day to dye. The niece didn't like this at all because she thought "dye" meant something else—"die." From that point on, Katherine says color instead of dye.

CANYON DE CHELLY

CANYON DE CHELLY is a national monument held in trust by the Navajo Nation and jointly managed by the National Park Service and the Navajo Nation. We call this canyon *Tséyí*, which means "inside the rock." Spider Rock, memorialized in the story of Spider Woman (see page 12) is located inside the canyon. There are families that live in the canyon, most of them seasonally. They farm and run livestock, and most take seasonal jobs such as driving, interpreting, and guiding tourists, who require a permit to enter most parts of the canyon.

Canyon de Chelly was a Navajo stronghold, the site of the Navajo Wars of 1864, the final major military engagement between the tribe and the United States government. At the end of the battle, the Navajos who were captured or surrendered were marched to Bosque Redondo in a series of four marches from different locations, marches of 300 to more than 400 miles. Navajos refer to these forced marches as "the Long Walk."

Manuelito and Barboncito led the Navajos in the canyon, and Kit Carson led the United States Army. Carson used a "scorched earth policy" to burn out the Navajo homesteads, their crops, orchards, and livestock. More than 9,500 Navajos were imprisoned and more than 2,000 perished. They were released after signing the Navajo Treaty of 1868. The unspeakable horrors of this historical trauma still permeate Navajos to this day, resulting in deep-rooted issues such as extreme poverty, dependence on the government, and other social ills.

Incredibly, as Navajos returned home, they held cleansing ceremonies and attempted to pick up their lives and find family members, and many survivors made it home to Canyon de Chelly.

FLORENCE NEZ RIGGS

TUBA CITY, ARIZONA

BORN OF THE DEER SPRING CLAN, *Bįįh Bitoodnii*

BORN FOR THE MEXICAN PEOPLE CLAN, *Naakaii Dine'é*

MOTHER'S FATHER, CLIFF DWELLING CLAN, *Tsé Ńjíkiní*

FATHER'S FATHER, ONE-WALKS-AROUND CLAN, *Honágháahnii*

Florence grew up in Sand Springs, Arizona, along with her siblings, Bill, Jane Nez Hyden, and LaVerne Nez Greyeyes. Her sisters are also renowned weavers. Florence and her husband, Perry Riggs Jr., raised four children: Adrian, Marietta, Averill, and Sean.

Florence's earlier childhood was spent on their homeland, but when she was sixteen, she moved with her family under a government relocation act. Florence's mother, Louise, and her father, Hosteen Nez, and their family were among the estimated 10,000 to 15,000 Navajo tribal members who were relocated in 1978.

The tentacles of this situation reach back to an 1882 presidential executive order under Chester Arthur, assigning two million acres of Navajo land for Moqui (Hopi) use. Almost a century of border disputes followed, and more than a century of court orders and congressional proposals have not been able to solve what is a complicated and still deeply emotional issue for both tribes. To further complicate matters,

FLORENCE SHOWS ONE OF TWO RUG DRESSES SHE WOVE FOR THE AUTHORS. THEY WORE THEM TO THE TINKUY INTERNATIONAL WEAVERS' CONFERENCE IN 2017. THRONGS OF INDIGENOUS WEAVERS FROM MANY COUNTRIES TOUCHED THE DRESSES WITH ADMIRATION; LYNDA AND BARBARA CONSIDERED THOSE TOUCHES TO BE BLESSINGS.

in the early 1960s, the Hopi tribe signed leases that allowed the Peabody Energy Corporation to drill for gas, oil, and minerals with approvals by the Bureau of Indian Affairs and the Navajo tribe for the coal royalty payments. This added player with monetary interests has further driven the division between the tribes, each of which regards their homelands as sacred to their culture and history.

Hearing the stories of her family's weaving history comforted and inspired her.

One of 3,500 Navajo families, the Nezes were uprooted from their homeland and ordered to sell their livestock, and moved to an area called New Lands, in northeastern Arizona, where they would have a house, land for livestock, a community hospital, and employment opportunities. Nahata Dziil Chapter was formed, but the area is now nothing but devastation.

The Nez family then moved to Flagstaff for a safer place to live, but the language barrier in this Anglo town prevented them from securing stable housing or employment, so they never got settled. They made another move to Farmington, New Mexico, for ten years of trying to fit in, but again, the language barrier prevented them from settling in long term, and Hosteen Nez passed on.

And so Florence saw the world through the eyes of a young girl experiencing tremendous turmoil, abiding by decisions made by the government and political leaders that did not make sense to her. She felt powerless. Years of living with her strong matriarchal family helped her make the best of her situation, though. Hearing the stories of her family's weaving history comforted and inspired her. Florence learned to weave from her mother and grandmother when she was eighteen years old. Her first rug was in the Two Grey Hills style.

But her grandmother's and her mother's pictorial weavings held the most interest for her. Florence searched for magazines, books, and any material that depicted life in the larger world—prehistoric, historic, and contemporary life. She has a wry sense of humor, which she brings to her style of picto-

rial weaving. She was inspired by the art she saw, by the trading post style of pictorial weaving that employed everything from cartoon characters to railroad trains; but when it comes to weaving her own pictorials, she lets her wide palette of wool colors and her personal imagery drive her creativity. She concentrates on the details of people and animal faces. She weaves her sense of humor into her lifestyle rugs.

In 2013, the Heard Museum's annual Indian Fair and Art Market chose the theme, "Weaving Worlds with Wool." As their signature artist, Florence was given the honor of weaving a pictorial to coincide with a pictorial weaving exhibit *Picture This*. Florence wove a pictorial titled "The Annual Indian Market." The rug is now in the Heard Museum's permanent collection. She has woven prehistoric scenes with dinosaurs, and a circus scene that can occupy one's attention for hours for its richness of detail.

In addition to showing and selling her weavings, Florence also teaches Navajo weaving at Diné College at its satellite location in Tuba City, further influencing aspiring young Navajo weavers.

Florence's work extends beyond her collectible rugs. She began a revival of personal rug dresses woven for girls and women graduating from high school or college, or for any other milestone in a Navajo woman's life. She designs each dress—and she has woven hundreds—with personality traits, school colors, and mascots in mind. One mind-blowing dress depicted elements from the Beatles' album cover of *Abbey Road* along with musical notes and the girl's last name on the back! Other weavers often copy her designs, but if you have an original Florence Riggs dress, it will have her initials, "FR," woven on the bottom.

Florence's weaving does indeed create quite a stir. It stirs up emotion, conversation, curiosity, and laughter, lots of laughter, and you walk away with an appreciation of a resilient Navajo weaver's view of the world.

OPPOSITE: LOUISE WOVE THIS STORM PATTERN RUG AS A GIFT FOR HER GRANDDAUGHTER—A VERY SPECIAL GESTURE, WHEN MOST NAVAJO WEAVERS SELL ALL THEIR RUGS FOR NEEDED INCOME.

LOUISE Y. NEZ
TUBA CITY, ARIZONA

BORN OF THE DEER SPRING CLAN, *Bįįh Bitoodnii*

BORN FOR THE CLIFF DWELLING CLAN, *Tsé Ńjíkiní*

MOTHER'S FATHER, TOWERING HOUSE CLAN, *Kinyaa'áanii*

FATHER'S FATHER, ONE-WALKS-AROUND CLAN, *Honágháahnii*

Louise lives next door to her daughter, Florence Riggs, near Tuba City. Before Louise's husband passed, he had been working on securing a homesite lease in Tuba City and making plans to have a house built. With that lease acquired, Louise, with her youngest son, made her final move, from Farmington to Tuba City. Louise learned to weave when she was eight years old. At eighty-five, she still weaves. Throughout all of her family's moves, the loss of their livestock, and the loss of their sacred homeland where the umbilical cords of several generations are buried, she maintained her motivation for weaving. Since she no longer has a flock of sheep, she is now using commercial wool, though for certain projects, she will buy roving to spin. She does use Churro wool for warp.

Louise weaves pictorials, very intricate pictorials that look like paintings, and has woven several Storm Pattern rugs for gifts to her grandchildren. Weaving rugs for gifts in highly unusual among the Navajo, as most rugs are woven to produce much-needed income. So a gift of a rug from a grandmother is truly a treasure.

Florence told the story about a man and his wife from Alabama who had visited the Utah national monuments and learned about her Tree of Life weavings. The man had been battling cancer and commissioned Louise to weave a Tree of Life rug for its healing message. By the time Louise finished weaving the rug, he had been cancer-free for three months. Louise said she wove the rug imbuing every strand of weft with healing thoughts. The man who commissioned the rug certainly thought this, and it seemed that Florence and her mom did, too. It is an important story for them.

IT BEGINS WITH THE SHEEP

THE SPANISH IMPORTED CHURRO sheep to southern Mexico in the fifteenth century, and within a hundred years, they had been brought north to the Navajo's lands. These sheep had a long, coarse outer coat and a softer, finer undercoat. They were distinctive looking, often bearing four horns. They were uniquely suited to the harsh climate of the American Southwest, and they thrived. In time, as the Navajo took up weaving, their wool supplanted cotton as the fiber of choice in that part of the world. It was ideal for sturdy rugs and blankets.

Soon, the Spanish introduced a new breed of sheep, the Merino, whose wool was uniformly fine and soft and greasy—more difficult to clean and prepare, but suitable for finer, softer textiles. Other breeds followed, all with the intent of "improving" the Churro. Given the wide-open ranges of the Navajo Nation, the different breeds interbred at will, and over time, most of the Churro characteristics were lost.

THE NAVAJO SHEEP PROJECT

In the 1970s, a group of conservationists led by Dr. Lyle McNeal collected a small flock of true Churros and began to breed them and by 1982 had begun disseminating them throughout the Navajo Nation and the rest of the country. Due to their efforts, there are now more than 5,000 registered animals in the program.

SHEEP IS LIFE: DIBÉ BÉ LINÁ

Since the mid-1990s, Navajo Lifeway has sponsored an annual event to celebrate the sheep and their place in Navajo culture. This event ties together all aspects of the sheep's role in Navajo culture, from sheepherding to food to spinning and weaving. It has been attended by sheep raisers from all over the world.

NAVAJO WOOL TODAY

Many Navajo weavers continue to prepare their yarn, from shearing to cleaning to spinning and dyeing and to weaving. Some are gathering their dyestuffs from the land. Rugs and blankets and tapestries made in this way command premium prices, as they should. But the labor involved in preparation can be too arduous for older weavers, or too time consuming for weavers needing to produce a piece quickly for the income. For them, there are other options.

BROWN SHEEP COMPANY

A family-owned mill in northern Nebraska has been producing yarns to Navajo weaving specifications for almost forty years. The wool comes from range sheep in Nebraska, Colorado, and Wyoming. "Top of the Lamb" yarns are spun in worsted and sport weights and a palette of a dozen hues; these single-ply yarns are readily available in the Navajo Nation. Many weavers "unspin" the yarns and respin them to a finer weight. Many also dye the white yarn to obtain special colors.

TAKING A RUG TO AUCTION

FOR WEAVERS WHO DON'T have established relationships with collectors or galleries, and who don't have access to the big sales venues such as Santa Fe Indian Market, or who simply want to raise some immediate cash, a rug auction can be a good resource.

We've attended two rug auctions in the past year, with mixed emotions. It's exciting to see the quality and number of rugs—often as many as two or three hundred—but it's heartbreaking to see how many don't sell. Sometimes as many as a third or even a half are taken back home, to be tried again another day. It's a game of chance: which buyers or dealers or collectors or random tourists show up. Will the big rugs be sought this time, or will the crowd go for small,

AN ABUNDANCE OF RUG SIZES AND STYLES ARE AVAILABLE AT THE CROWNPOINT RUG AUCTION, AN IMPORTANT SALES VENUE FOR AREA WEAVERS.

more affordable pieces? Will they reward the rugs that are traditional, handspun and naturally dyed, or will they be excited by innovative colors and designs?

The Hubbell Trading Post hosts two big auctions each year, spring and fall, in Gallup, New Mexico. Crownpoint, New Mexico, about sixty miles farther north, has auctions on the second Friday of each month.

The Crownpoint Rug Auction has been in existence for almost fifty years. It was formerly under the management of the late Lavonne and Bill Palmer, owners of the Crownpoint Trading Post (now just a filling station and convenience store), but in 2014, the Navajo Rug Weavers' Association of Crownpoint took over management of the auction.

The auction takes place in the Crownpoint Elementary School's gymnasium, with weavers beginning to queue up to check in their rugs at 3:00 p.m. The weavers set minimum prices for the bidding on their rugs.

Weavers from all over the Navajo Nation bring their rugs, and there is time for the customers to see the rugs on tables and for the weavers to visit with each other. Vendors have tables, selling crafts and supplies, and a kitchen crew does a brisk business making and selling Navajo tacos and fry bread.

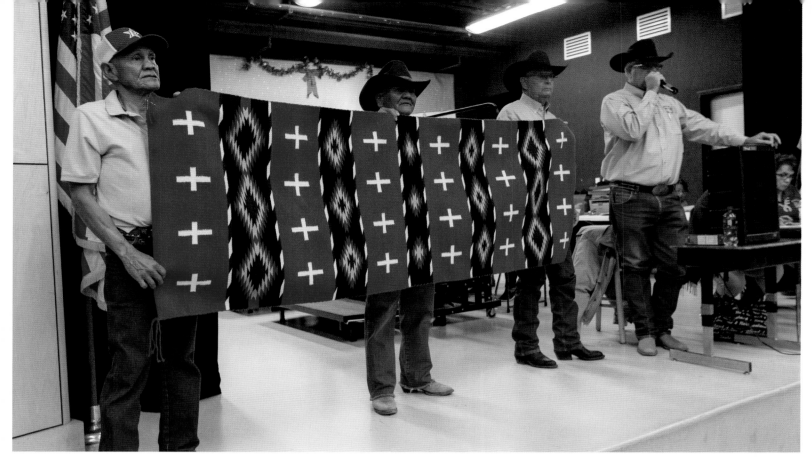

SEVERAL HUNDRED RUGS GO ON THE BLOCK AT A TYPICAL AUCTION.

The auction starts around 7:00 p.m. and ends when all the rugs have been held up for auction. But before the bidding begins, at the auction we attended, the woman who heads the Rug Association spoke to the crowd about the importance of retaining the language of the Diné. She led the crowd in singing a birthday song in Navajo and delivered a prayer, also in Navajo. The crowd honored veterans with the Pledge of Allegiance. She thanked the weavers for coming, and sincerely encouraged them to bring their rugs back another time if they didn't sell. This genuine gesture softened the heartbreak of watching so many weavers retrieve their unsold rugs.

One of the weavers, Louise Tsosie (see page 83), brought a handsome rug of red, black, gray, and white stripes with bands of Chinle stars that she had woven in just a week's time. It sold for the price she had set, and she commented that she would sleep well that night. The Crownpoint auction is a good outlet for weavers to sell their work.

With beauty below me I walk.

WEAVING IN THE 21ST CENTURY

TODAY'S YOUNG NAVAJO weavers represent a new generation which is not tied to trading post styles of weaving. Buoyed perhaps by ancestral memory, new weavers today make the transition from learning basic technique to incorporating other artistic media and new imagery into their work. They are telling their own survival stories. They are bold in pushing the boundaries of traditional weaving, and impressive at using today's technology and knowledge to advance their adventurous weaving styles—and to sell them.

And what does this mean for the future of Navajo weaving? As more young people have access to higher education and greater employment opportunities, there's a natural migration away from remote family homes on the reservation to urban jobs and apartments. Those who leave the reservation, while they may continue to have deep ties to their families and ancestral homes, find themselves surrounded by new landscapes and new cultural influences. Reflecting these new influences in their weaving is only natural. It's a continuation, in its own way, of the constant evolution that Navajo weaving has always experienced, from the eighteenth century to contemporary times.

A fortunate reality that can help sustain the art is that it has come to have great value in the marketplace. Tapestries, whether traditional or modern, can command high prices if they are well designed and well made. There's still a career path for weavers who aim to excel.

AILLA TELLER RESTS AGAINST A ROCK WALL AT THE EDGE OF HER FAMILY'S LAND IN CANON DE CHELLY. FIRMLY ROOTED IN HER NAVAJO TRADITIONS, AILLA LOOKS TO THE FUTURE.

VELMA KEE CRAIG

MESA, ARIZONA

BORN OF THE ZUNI WATER'S EDGE CLAN, *Naasht'ézhí*
Tábąąhá Dine'é

BORN FOR THE BITTER WATER CLAN, *Tódích'íi'nii*

MOTHER'S FATHER, MANY GOATS CLAN, *Tł'ízí Łání*

FATHER'S FATHER, TOWERING HOUSE PEOPLE, *Kinyaa'áanii*

Velma Craig's childhood was marked by frequent moves. She moved with her parents, Laverne Marks Mandia and Larry Kee, from Tonalea, to Page, to Fort Defiance, to Klagetoh, and back to Fort Defiance where her parents were finally able to establish a permanent home for themselves and their four children. In Tonalea, Velma's family stayed with her maternal grandmother, Elva Marks. Velma watched her grandmother process wool; she herded and cared for the sheep, sheared the wool, carded, washed, and dyed the wool. As family members shared stories, Velma learned that her grandmother was also a weaver. There are a few old photos of her holding up a finished textile. Velma inherited her grandmother's weaving tools.

During fourth grade, Velma's family moved over to her father's side of the reservation and lived briefly with her paternal grandparents. Her grandmother wove all the time while the grandchildren watched television and played nearby. This is a lasting memory that Velma treasures, the time spent

VELMA KEE CRAIG IS A CONTEMPORARY FACE OF NAVAJO ART. THIS PHOTOGRAPH AND THE ONES OF HER CHILDREN WERE TAKEN WITH PERMISSION AT THE HEARD MUSEUM IN PHOENIX, ARIZONA.

watching her grandmother weave. She enjoyed the methodical movements of her grandmother's hands and fell in love with the sounds of weaving and the warm, earthy smells of the sheep.

After graduating from Window Rock High School in 1995, Velma earned her BA in English literature from Arizona State University in Tempe, and is working towarda master's degree in creative writing. In the meantime, she is learning museum and library studies (emphasis in textile conservation and long-term care) as an Andrew Mellon Fellow at the Heard Museum in Phoenix. The time finally came for Velma to make weaving a part of her life. She and her daughter Ashlee took a two-week class with Barbara and me at the Idyllwild Arts Academy in 2010 (see page 107), and weaving began to take off for her. Her first weaving was sold to the Heard Museum. Up until this point, she says, "I was very timid in trying to market myself as a weaver. I didn't weave full-time or quickly. I was still unsure about my skill level and didn't have as much confidence as I thought I should have."

Now Velma sells her work through social media and through the stories she tells on her blog *Warped Canvas*, http://warpedcanvas.blogspot.com/. She's currently working on a rug design based on the *Finding Nemo* movie that has been dubbed in Navajo.

Velma's journey back to Navajo weaving took a while, but once she immersed herself in learning, she wanted to teach other Navajos like herself. She says, "I love teaching! Especially, because my students are primarily Navajo. I have

THIS RUG, TITLED QR CODE, CAUSES THE VIEWER TO DO A DOUBLE TAKE. THE IRONY SPEAKS LOUD AND CLEAR.

been lucky to fall into working for organizations that have received funding for cultural revitalization and education. Every student comes to the class with a different level of knowledge of the techniques and the philosophy and history of weaving, and of Navajo culture in general. They are diverse in their understanding and in their beliefs, even though we are all Navajo.

"I think they appreciate that I, too, am a classroom learner. This makes them less self-conscious. I encourage them to share with others the knowledge they bring and also their stories. I also encourage them to encourage one another. I tell them they are part of a weaving culture. They will leave this classroom with the understanding that they will seek knowledge from other weavers beyond me, from their elder family members. I tell them weaving is a continual learning journey. They must also be willing to accept help and critique. So far,

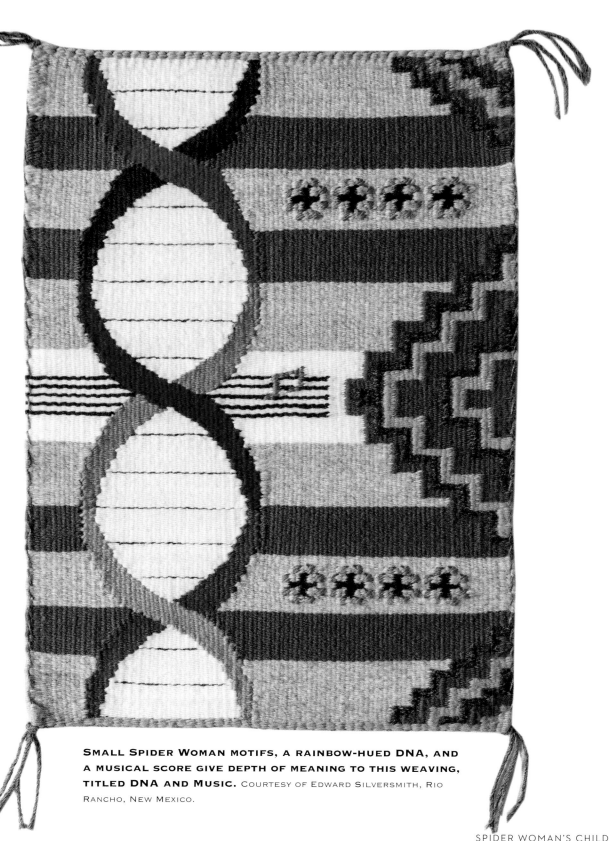

SMALL SPIDER WOMAN MOTIFS, A RAINBOW-HUED DNA, AND A MUSICAL SCORE GIVE DEPTH OF MEANING TO THIS WEAVING, TITLED DNA AND MUSIC. COURTESY OF EDWARD SILVERSMITH, RIO RANCHO, NEW MEXICO.

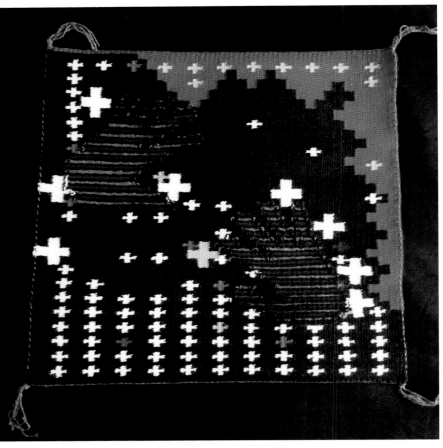

ABOVE LEFT: THIS PIECE IS TITLED YAA' ET' EEH, THE COMMON GREETING WHEN TWO PEOPLE MEET. ACCENT STRIPES OF USED AUDIOTAPE IMPLY A LIVELY CONVERSATION.

RIGHT: CROSS MOTIFS TO HONOR HER FATHER, AND A VIDEO GAME MOTIF JUST FOR FUN SHOW THE CULTURAL INTERSECTIONS IN ASHLEE'S APPROACH TO WEAVING.

they have been. We have all become more humble on this journey."

Because of the nomadic lifestyle her family experienced in her early years, Velma did not know the styles that her grandmothers wove. Essentially, this has given her the freedom to weave rugs about herself, her discoveries, and her dreams; it allows her to infuse her artistic voice in the weavings to make sense of the world. She has the freedom to create abstract contemporary styles and maybe mix in a touch of trading post styles—or not!

Velma lives in Mesa with her four children, Kraig, Chance, Ashlee, and Tristan.

ASHLEE MARIE AND TRISTAN CRAIG
MESA, ARIZONA

BORN OF THE ZUNI WATER'S EDGE CLAN, *Naasht'ézhí Tábąąhá Dine'é*

BORN FOR THE WHITE MOUNTAIN APACHE, *Biltsoon*

MOTHER'S FATHER, BITTER WATER CLAN, *Tódích'íi'nii*

FATHER'S FATHER, WEAVERS-ZIA CLAN, *Tł'ógí*

Ashlee Marie Craig was born in Pinetop, Arizona, in 1998 to Velma and Dustinn Craig. Ashlee attended the Navajo weaving class at Idyllwild Arts Academy with her mother

A PLACE TO LEARN

THE IDYLLWILD ARTS ACADEMY was founded in 1947 with the mission of "changing lives through the transformative power of art." Set in the San Jacinto Mountains southwest of Los Angeles, the school comprises a residential high school and a robust summer program that serves more than 2,000 attendees. The school offers several Native American Teacher/Community Leader Scholarships for adults eighteen and over with current tribal affiliation. The purpose of this fund is to bring teachers and community leaders to workshops at Idyllwild Arts that will benefit not only those individuals but also students in their home schools and communities. Applicants with financial need are given priority. They do accept children with a parent, and that is how Velma and her daughter Ashlee first came to Idyllwild to take a Navajo weaving class in 2010.

Barbara started teaching Navajo weaving at the Idyllwild Arts Academy in 1997, and Lynda joined her in 2000.

as a library assistant while attending Mesa Community College in Mesa, Arizona.

Ashlee's brother Tristan is four years younger, the youngest child in his family. Tristan attended the Navajo weaving class at Idyllwild Arts with his mother, also when he was twelve years old. He says he thought the weaving workshop

TRISTAN CRAIG BRINGS THE ENTHUSIASM OF YOUTH TO HIS WEAVING, AS IN THE "SMILEY FACE" WEAVING BELOW.

when she was twelve years old, and thought it was empowering. She enjoyed learning to weave; the experience was very special to her, especially since it is a part of her culture as a Navajo woman. The most special part was removing the weaving from the loom, cutting the selvedge cords representing the umbilical cords. It was a reward and a blessing to see something she created and put so much work into come off the loom, and the blessing that followed was especially touching and meaningful.

The design for her first weaving had a cross motif. She wanted to make something for her father, who is an artist. He uses the same type of crosses that she incorporated into her first weaving in his drawings and signature logos to mark the designs he creates. Ashlee is an avid painter, loves to skateboard, and is currently working at the Tempe Public Library

in Idyllwild was cool. He remembers sitting in a room full of older women and hearing their banter. This was enjoyable. His first weaving was a pictorial, a smiley face. He wove it because it was fun, for him and for those who would see it. He was a fast weaver and started a second rug in class. Life drawing and photography are his hobbies, and he is a sophomore at the New School for the Arts and Academics, a charter school in Tempe, Arizona.

FULL CIRCLE: SEVEN GENERATIONS

THROUGHOUT SEVEN GENERATIONS of our family's history, we have been able to provide for, support, and inspire each other with our weavings. We are not alone; many other families in the Navajo Nation have similar stories to tell. When, as a people, our lands were taken, when our flocks were taken, when our homes were taken, when our crops were burned, we still had the means to weave. We had wood for looms and tools. If we had no sheep, we unraveled old cloth to obtain fiber to re-spin. We had the patterns passed down through our family; we had the songs and prayers.

In our own time, our weaving has come to be valued, sought out by collectors, honored in public museums and galleries. Along with the hundreds of Navajos we have taught, hundreds of non-Navajos have taken our weaving classes as well, learning to better understand the skills and spirit inherent in our work.

In the beginning of this book, you learned of our mother, our grandmothers, and our aunts who taught us. Here at the end, we share who we are today, how we practice our art, how we endeavor to pass it on to the next generation.

ROSANN TELLER LEE

BORN TO THE WATER'S EDGE CLAN, *Tábąąhá*

BORN FOR THE WATER-FLOWS-TOGETHER CLAN, *Tó'aheedlíinii*

MOTHER'S FATHER, RED BOTTOM PEOPLE, *Tł'ááshchí'í*

FATHER'S FATHER, ONE-WALKS-AROUND CLAN, *Honágháahnii*

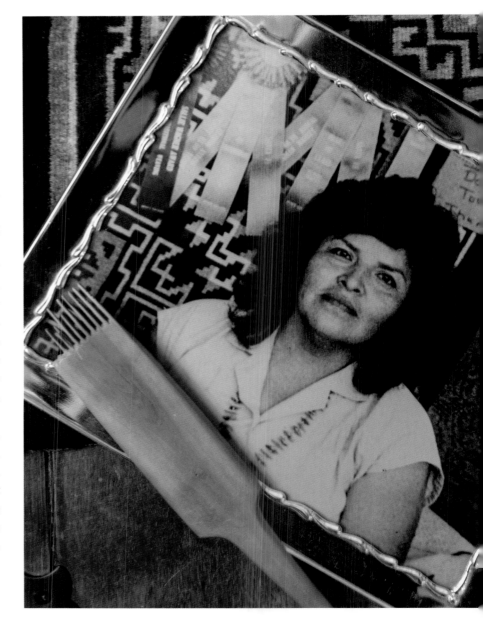

Rosann was the oldest child of our parents, Ruth and Sam Teller, and was born in 1945 at Tohatchi, New Mexico. She passed on in 1996. She attended Santa Fe Boarding School and graduated from Albuquerque High School, in Albuquerque, New Mexico. She attended Haskell Junior College in Lawrence, Kansas, where she was a year away from graduating with a nursing degree when she contracted tuberculosis and spent a year in a hospital in Albuquerque. It was at the hospital that she learned all kinds of crafts: needlepoint, embroidery, beadwork, crocheting, knitting, and quilting. As children, we were unable to visit her, but we would get gifts that she made. After her recovery, she took employment in Kayenta, Arizona, and did not finish her degree.

Rosann learned how to weave from our mother, Ruth, and her paternal grandmother, Nellie Peshlaki Teller. Rosann spent a lot of time with Nellie when she was young, and in between her school and work life. She learned a lot about the history of the Navajo's struggles after they came home from the Long Walk in 1868. She learned the weaving songs and prayers for every step of weaving. Lynda and I refer to

IN THIS THIRTY-YEAR-OLD PHOTOGRAPH, ROSANN SITS IN FRONT OF THE LARGEST, FINEST TAPESTRY ON RECORD. NOTE THE WEAR AND TEAR ON HER COMB. SHE DIDN'T HOLD BACK.

our mother, Ruth, and our aunts Margaret and Mary Louise (pages 21 and 26) as troubleshooters for weaving issues, but when they got into situations, they went to Rosann. She was that clever. Most of our weaving relatives and even weavers from outside our community sought her out. Our mother said Rosann's mind was quick; she would show her a weaving technique only once and next thing, Rosann would think of a better way to do it, taking it to the next level.

In 1969, Rosann married Larry Lee and raised three sons, Larry Jr., Terry, and Gary Bo. Larry Jr. served in the U.S. Marines and Terry served in the U.S. Army. While raising a family, Rosann took on other employment; she worked at the Two Grey Hills Trading Post with our father, Sam, and our brother Ernest. She learned all about marketing rugs and freely gave advice to other weavers on how to improve their work and get better prices. She learned how to drive a school bus as a challenge from her husband, who drove Newcomb School buses. She became an expert driver, and she was the only driver unafraid to navigate the mountains in snowy conditions. She drove the school buses part-time, and she had part-time jobs at the Newcomb Trading Post and briefly at Toadlena Trading Post. In addition to her part-time jobs, she made custom clothes, wedding cakes, and wedding dresses for area customers. In her off times, she still wove at home. She was the first weaver we knew who had multiple tapestries set up, from large, medium, and small to miniature. Now that is a standard practice for us. She processed her own wool, handcarding and spinning her weft and warp. We regarded her as the best weaver in our family. Rosann was a master Two Grey Hills weaver. Her Two Grey Hills designs were incredible, so intricate, and in her miniature tapestries, she wove one-warp designs so fine that people thought they were needlepoint work.

When Lynda and I were kids, we sat at a double loom, face-to-face. Rosann would come in with her yardstick and her measuring tape and check our progress. She would make us take our woven areas out if she thought we could do better. We called her "The General," and when she walked away, Lynda and I would playfully do a mock salute to her.

But without her quality-control patrol, we wouldn't be the weavers we are today.

Rosann won numerous awards, mostly first-place ribbons and several "Best of Shows" in our regional area: Gallup Inter-Tribal Ceremonial, Shiprock Northern Navajo Nation Fair, Window Rock Navajo Nation Fair, New Mexico State Fair. I assisted her entrance into the Santa Fe Indian Market in 1987 when we did a huge collaborative project together.

Before she entered the art market, Rosann sold exclusively to area trading posts and forged good relationships with the traders, even though she was outspoken about the quality of

We regarded her as the best weaver in our family. Her Two Grey Hills designs were incredible, so intricate, and in her miniature tapestries, she wove one-warp designs so fine that people thought they were needlepoint work.

her work and firmly set her prices, maybe to the chagrin of some of the traders. The traders did pay her firm prices because they knew they could sell her work with a high profit margin. Collectors especially sought her miniature tapestries. She won the Best of Show at Gallup Ceremonial with one of her miniatures, for which they had to create a miniature category.

Rosann, my mother, and I (Barbara) were concerned about the economic slowdown in the early 1980s, and we worried about not selling the smaller tapestries we were making. We decided to do a very large Two Grey Hills tapestry—8½ by 5 feet—all woven with handcarded, handspun wool warp and weft.

Our weaving sessions, sitting side by side, were among the best times of my life. Because of her busy daytime work schedule, we used to sit together weaving late at night. While weaving, we would tell each other our dreams—what we wanted for ourselves after this tapestry was finished. Rosann wanted a big house to raise her boys and a large space for weaving. Rosann was nine years older than me, and I really got to know her during this time. The only thing I remember of her personality before we wove the big rug was that she was so bossy! But I found out what a wonderful person she was, and we became close friends. She was always full of hope. She wanted a better future for herself and her boys. She was a very hard worker and not everyone could hold three jobs, take care of her family, and still make time to weave.

The big rug took four years to complete, and in 1987 we entered it in the Santa Fe Indian Market. It took first place, Best of Classification, Best of Division, and the special Sally Wagner Award, and it was the first time in Santa Fe Indian Market's sixty-six-year history that a weaving had won Best of Show. On the morning of the first day of Indian Market, we collected our tapestry with all the ribbons hanging off, and we walked through the Santa Fe historic plaza, heading to our booth on Lincoln Avenue. Navajo artists came out of their booths to clap and cheer, and several came up to us and said they were so proud to be Navajos, shaking our hands or hugging us. We sold the tapestry for 60,000 dollars! Rosann got her wish; she bought a house to raise her boys in with space for her weaving, and I bought my house in Tucson, Arizona.

I will forever be grateful that I spent this time with her and learned so much about weaving techniques that I am passing on to my sister Lynda, my children Sierra and Michael, my granddaughter Roxanne, and in his time, my grandson Javier.

In the years following the big rug, Rosann continued to weave fine tapestries. It was her high weft count achieved by spinning her weft very thin, basically threadlike, that gave her weaving skills their fame. Her weft counts were consistently above 120 wefts per inch.

We lost her, her son Bo, and her grandson Terrance in a terrible accident that sent our family into the darkest period of our lives. None of us wove. After a year had gone by, our mother called us home to Newcomb and she gave us Rosann's weaving tools. She said, "You need to weave, put your grief and your happy memories into your work. Rosann would want you to weave, she wanted you all to be the best

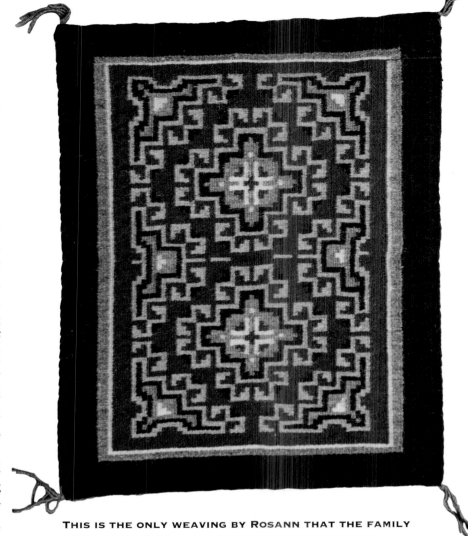

THIS IS THE ONLY WEAVING BY ROSANN THAT THE FAMILY OWNS. HER WORK HAS GONE OUT INTO THE WORLD.

weavers you can be." Now when I am challenged, I reach for Rosann's or my mother's weaving tools; I use them or hold them and let the tools give me the energy I need to continue weaving. The world lost a great weaver, but her legacy continues on with Lynda, Sierra, Michael, Roxanne, Javier and future grandchildren, and me.

BARBARA TELLER ORNELAS

TUCSON, ARIZONA

BORN TO THE WATER'S EDGE CLAN, *Tábąąhá*

BORN FOR THE WATER-FLOWS-TOGETHER CLAN, *Tó'aheedlíinii*

MOTHER'S FATHER, RED BOTTOM PEOPLE, *Tł'ááshchí'í*

FATHER'S FATHER, ONE-WALKS-AROUND CLAN, *Honágháahnii*

Lynda says: My sister Barbara was the middle child of our parents, Sam and Ruth Teller. Our mother began teaching her to weave when she was six years old. At the time, she disliked it and says it felt like taking piano lessons. She sold her first rug to the Two Grey Hills Trading Post at age ten for 10 dollars. She remembers the rug was shaped like an hourglass, but she was proud of it.

Barbara was born in the shadow of our older sister, Rosann, who had a big personality. Barbara was quiet and sedate in comparison, but I've always said she "walks softly but carries a big stick." That "stick" is her outsized weaving talent. She is noted for her exquisite Two Grey Hills tapestries with very high weft counts, from 110 to 122 wefts per inch, but she also weaves other styles with the same high weft counts. When she served as Artist in Residence at the Heard Museum from 1984 to 1988, she learned to step outside her comfort zone and weave many styles of rug. She became known for Burntwater tapestries, with their soft, vegetal-dyed colors, and for miniatures, among others. A series of her miniature First, Second, and Third Phase Chief Blankets can be found in many museums

WEAVING, TEACHING, LOOKING AFTER FAMILY, AND MORE WEAVING MAKE UP BARBARA'S LIFE.

Barbara's workroom is full of working projects, future projects, inspiration, and materials.

around the country. She has been a trailblazer, opening doors for the rest of us.

When Barbara was small and sitting at the loom that our paternal grandmother, Nellie Peshlaki Teller, had set up for her, Nellie would watch her weave and she would say to Barbara, "You were born to be a weaver. I had a dream that you will travel the world and tell people about our work. You will be a great weaver. I saw you on a big plane and talking to lots of people." All these years later, Barbara has reaped almost every weaving award imaginable and has traveled and taught in Uzbekistan and Kyrgyzstan, and in Peru three times, representing the U.S. government, the Navajo people, and the art of Navajo weaving.

Her first trip abroad was with a group of Native American artists who were invited to be in residence at the British Museum in London. Her whole family went, even Michael, who was just a baby. A very special milestone for Navajo children is the occasion of their first laugh, which is marked with a big party, friends and relatives coming from all over. Well, Michael delivered his first laugh there at the museum, and a party with all the museum employees, plus a Japanese band playing American country music, ensued. Family and career have always been closely intertwined in Barbara's life.

Barbara generally works at least eight to twelve hours a day, six days a week. Just before the annual Heard Museum's Indian Fair and Art Market and the Santa Fe Indian Market, she is up and working even longer hours, as those markets are important sources of income.

Barbara receives commissions for tapestries in regional styles such as Ganado and Burntwater, and styles from the Classic Revival period including Moqui, children's blankets, and women's mantas. She weaves enormous tapestries, and she weaves miniatures. She has even been known to weave complete outfits for "Navajo Barbie," authentic down to the smallest detail (except, of course, for Barbie's shape, which is not that of a typical Navajo woman). No piece goes unsold, and some collectors give her a retainer during the months it might take to complete a large piece. At home, Barbara has shoeboxes stuffed with a lot of Best of Class and Best of Division awards, and many specialty awards, and her work is in museums and private collections all over the world. There's a great amount of emotion involved in each finished piece. Her tapestries are like her children; she has a select group of collectors who buy her work and give her visiting privileges. She's comforted in knowing they are in loving places and treasured. "It's a special joy for me to meet the people who will buy my work," she says.

But almost as important as her weaving is her teaching. Barbara gives generously of her time to demonstrate, judge, and curate. "I never say no," she says. The two of us teach together all over the country, and most especially at the Idyllwild School of Arts in Idyllwild, California. There, every summer, we teach Navajos and other Native Americans who attend on scholarship, and non-natives as well. Sometimes the scholarships are granted to two generations of a family, and teaching a mother-daughter or mother-son pair is particularly rewarding because we feel we are teaching for the

future. And we love teaching in Canyon de Chelly at least once a year.

This seems like an ambitious and progressive career for a weaver who did not want to be a weaver as a child, doesn't it? But Barbara says, "My work, my ideas, my processes and weaving materials are ever evolving, but stay true to the standards set by my elders. I take the responsibility of carrying on our family's tradition by teaching my family and mentoring others to help preserve this cultural legacy."

BARBARA'S COLLECTION OF SHEEP COMES FROM ALL OVER THE WORLD, AND TAKES ITS PLACE BESIDE FAMILY PHOTOS AND DWIGHT YOAKAM CDS. (A MAJOR FAN, SHE HAS ATTENDED MORE THAN 150 OF HIS CONCERTS.)

LYNDA TELLER PETE

DENVER, COLORADO

BORN TO THE WATER'S EDGE CLAN, *Tábąąhá*

BORN FOR THE WATER-FLOWS-TOGETHER CLAN, *Tó'aheedlíinii*

MOTHER'S FATHER, RED BOTTOM PEOPLE, *Tł'ááshchí'í*

FATHER'S FATHER, ONE-WALKS-AROUND CLAN, *Honágháahnii*

Barbara says: My sister Lynda is the youngest in our family. Our father was working at Buffalo Springs Trading Post north of Gallup when she was born. He was teaching a new trader the business. Lynda was taught the art of weaving by our mother, Ruth Teller; she also learned the techniques and designs from our sister Rosann. Because she was the youngest, she wasn't allowed to go with us to stay at our grandparents' place in White Rock, New Mexico, so she didn't get to spend as much time with our paternal grandmother, Nellie Peshlaki Teller. So our sister Rosann and I taught her the stories, the songs, and prayers we learned from our grandmother.

Lynda wove a small Two Grey Hills rug when she was around the age of twelve. Our mother entered it in the Gallup Inter-Tribal Ceremonial for judging, and she won first place. Looking back, I think she was the very first person in our family to win a ribbon. Rosann and I went on to become professional weavers, but Lynda took the academic road. She graduated from Arizona State University in Tempe, moved to Denver, and went to work for the government. She was in the workforce for more than twenty years. What she learned on the job she still uses to this day in our weaving business.

LIKE HER SISTERS' TAPESTRIES, LYNDA'S TEND TO BE VERY FINE, OFTEN RUNNING UP TO 120 WEFTS PER VERTICAL INCH.

Even when she is weaving the traditional Two Grey Hills, her work overflows with her own creativity, added color, and intricate patterns.

When we lost our sister Rosann in 1996, we went through a very dark period. Our mom somehow managed to come out of her grief long enough to give us our sister's tools and said, "We need to be strong as a family and keep weaving." I know Lynda took that to heart; she had stopped weaving for a long time and this is what brought her back. I remember looking at my children and watching them weave, thinking, "This is it. There's no one else to carry this forward." I told Lynda this, and she really worked hard to relearn her weaving. She puts her whole heart into every project she does, one hundred percent. If you visit her home in Denver, you can see the ties to family and tradition. Everywhere you see tools, looms with work in progress, skeins of yarn reaching for the perfect shade of blue. Holding pride of place is the last rug our mother wove. She wove one for each of her four children before she lost her strength. Lynda got the last rug; it's the only one that doesn't have a Weaver's Path to lead to the next rug. Our mother knew this was her last one.

I asked Lynda to help me with a Navajo weaving class at the Idyllwild School of Arts in the late 1990s. She wasn't sure if she could do it, but using the tools she had acquired in her job, she became a great teacher, an amazing teacher. She is very patient with our students, teaching them from the beginning to the finishing of their weaving process, explaining along the way the reasons why we do things and equating the process with something they can relate to if they are weavers of a different type. She is great at encouraging them to do their best when the weaving process gets challenging.

Lynda is also very talented in beadwork; she juried in as a beadworker at Santa Fe Indian Market before she juried in

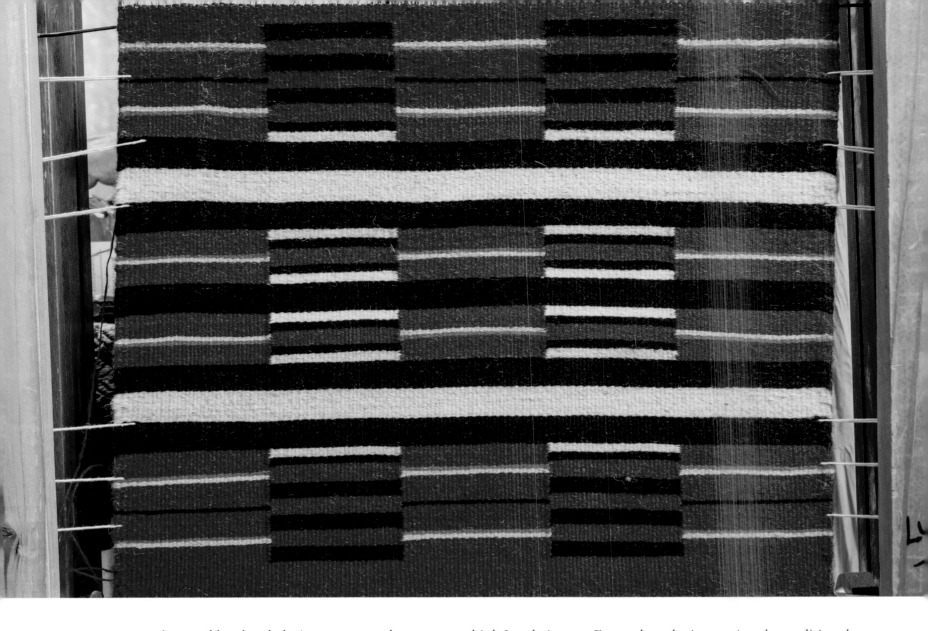

as a weaver, and one of her beaded pieces was on the cover of *Beadwork* magazine. But I kept at her to enter one of her weavings. It took a while, but when she entered, there was no turning back. She won first place with a Two Grey Hills tapestry on her first entry. I was so proud of her. Another weaver came over to me and said, "You won again, huh?" I told her, "No, it's my sister Lynda this time." She replied with a surprised look, "There's another one of you?" I replied with the biggest smile, "Yes, and she will be one of the great ones." And so she is, and the awards she has garnered show it.

Our grandmother used to call me a "born weaver," but I think Lynda is, too. Even when she is weaving the traditional Two Grey Hills, her work overflows with her own creativity, added color, and intricate patterns. I encouraged her a little, but once she started, she was well on her way. Lynda is younger than me, but we have been best friends since she was born. We have built a great business of teaching Navajo weaving and being weaving partners. I couldn't ask for a better friend and sister. There's nothing I love better than driving down the road in the middle of the night after a long day of teaching, listening to the music we both love, on our way to our next weaving class.

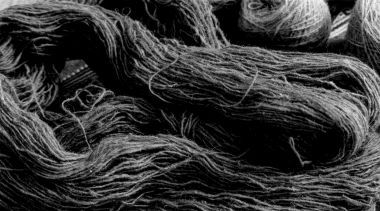

OPPOSITE: A MINIATURE TAPESTRY BASED ON THIRD PHASE CHIEF'S BLANKET DESIGNS.

ABOVE LEFT: ONE OF LYNDA'S PROJECTS IN PROGRESS IS A TWO GREY HILLS USING THE TURQUOISE AND GOLD ACCENTS THAT WERE PREVALENT DURING THE MID-1950S, WHEN WILLARD LEIGHTON OWNED THE TRADING POST. AFTER HIS DEMISE, THE STYLE WENT BACK TO ALL-NATURAL COLORS.

WORKING WITH DONNA BROWN, DYE EXPERT WITH THE DENVER BOTANIC GARDENS, LYNDA STRIVES TO FIND THE PERFECT VEGETAL-DYED BLUE.

LYNDA AND HER HUSBAND OF TWENTY-SEVEN YEARS, BELVIN PETE, FIND SYNERGY BETWEEN HER TEACHING AND HIS TOOL MAKING.

BELVIN E. PETE

DENVER, COLORADO

BORN OF THE ARROW PEOPLE CLAN, *K'aa' Dine'é*

BORN FOR THE RED BOTTOM PEOPLE, *Tł'ááshchí'í*

MOTHER'S FATHER, MANY HOGANS CLAN, *Hooghan Łání*

FATHER'S FATHER, TANGLE PEOPLE, *Ta'neeszahnii*

BELVIN PETE USES HIS TRAINING AS A MECHANICAL ENGINEER TO GOOD USE IN DESIGNING TOOLS THAT BEST DO THEIR JOB.

Belvin grew up in Dzilth-na-o-dith-hle, New Mexico, youngest of five siblings. His parents were Wilfred and Ruth Pete. Ruth was a jeweler, weaver, and weaving teacher, and his father served in two military branches before returning home to work for the Utah International Navajo Mine.

Belvin's parents and his maternal grandmother had a huge flock of sheep, as well as cattle and horses. Belvin's chores after school and during summers were to work with the livestock. One summer, his mother wanted a new weaving comb and showed him and his brother how they were made. After understanding how his mother liked her tools, he continued to make tools all summer. Soon thereafter, his paternal aunts also ordered tools.

After high school, and eager to get away from the livestock chores, Belvin attended and graduated from New Mexico State University in Las Cruces with a B.S. in mechanical engineering. After finding employment in Denver and marrying Lynda, Belvin had to dust off his tools to make weaving tools for his in-law weaving family. Lynda taught her way of weaving to Belvin, which led him to design some unique looms for the entire Teller weaving family. He designed a collapsible loom that can be broken down with a current weaving project attached, rolled up, wrapped, and put into a tube, ready to travel by plane or car. At the destination, it can be set up in less than ten minutes. Just adjust the tension and you are ready to weave.

For our Navajo weaving classes, he designed a basic classroom loom in two sizes for students to warp and weave on the same loom. Belvin has created a tabletop attachment so that students do not have to sit on the floor or adjust the height of their chairs. The loom can be adjusted to eye level to alleviate back and neck pain. The loom and attachments are very versatile, portable, strong, and durable—but it is still a traditional Navajo upright vertical loom. Belvin also makes custom looms in a variety of woods and styles. Now he has started making Navajo lap spindles, with particular attention to making sure they are perfectly balanced—and to how they will be used.

Most of the weavers we talk to today like to spin as pas-

sengers in their vehicles. Our mother used to spin in our family's pickup as our father drove. She used to draft the wool right under his nose, trying to make him sneeze. He would be unfazed, driving, changing gears, and blowing air out of his nose or mouth to keep the wool away from his face. Belvin has designed a small spindle for those who like to spin in the passenger seat of a moving vehicle—without endangering the driver!

TOOLMAKERS

NA' ASHJÉII ASDZÁÁ, SPIDER WOMAN, gave the gift of weaving to Navajo people. Spider Man made the weaving loom, spindles, and weaving tools.

Historically, Diné men were makers of weaving looms and tools, although currently, gender roles are not so closely defined. An early memory I have of my mother is watching her weave very large tapestries. When she was near finishing, she would look for thinner battens that would pass through the final tight warps. Finding none, she would pack up her knife and gloves and walk to a big arroyo about a half mile from our Two Grey Hills apartment behind the Post. In the arroyo were tall thin tamarisks, and she would select several straight branches, cut them down, and strip the barks. Smoothing the branches with her gloved hands, she would walk home and continue with her weaving. It was a quick fix to solve her weaving challenge, and she was self-reliant. With each new tool made or designed, a song and a prayer are offered to work in beauty with the weaver to create rugs in harmony.

In our visits to Navajo weavers, invariably they brought out their weaving tools. Many were handed down by parents, grandparents, relatives, or from medicine people. The tools looked well taken care of, cherished, and ready to be passed on to the younger weavers, along with the legacy, the stories, the songs, and the prayers.

TERRY B. LEE

TUCSON, ARIZONA

BORN OF THE WATER'S EDGE PEOPLE, *Tábąąhá*

BORN FOR THE RED BOTTOM PEOPLE, *Tł'ááshchí'í*

MOTHER'S FATHER, WATER-FLOWS-TOGETHER CLAN,
Tó'aheedlíinii

FATHER'S FATHER, RED-RUNNING-INTO-THE-WATER CLAN,
Táchii'nii

TERRY LEE, SON OF ROSANN TELLER LEE AND FATHER OF ROXANNE, PRODUCES CUSTOM TOOLS AND LARGE NUMBERS OF WORKSHOP LOOMS IN HIS COMPACT WORKSHOP.

Terry Lee, the middle son of master Navajo weaver, Rosann Teller Lee and Larry Lee, grew up in Newcomb, New Mexico, on the Navajo Nation surrounded by Navajo weavers, toolmakers, and sheep raisers. Terry, as an early budding artist, favored comic book art and excelled at pencil drawings in school. Artists who have influenced him range from Vincent van Gogh to Kurt Cobain.

After a stint in the U.S. Army, Terry attended the Art Center Design College of Tucson, specializing in character design rigging for animations. Before finishing his degree program, Terry's wife, also a soldier, was transferred to Fort Lewis in Tacoma, Washington. Uprooting the entire blended family, they moved to the Seattle/Tacoma area and Terry enrolled in the Art Institute of Seattle. Terry's focus was on a bachelor's degree in 3D animation. Terry, now a single father of then ten-year-old Roxanne, moved back to Tucson before he was able to acquire his art degree in Seattle.

Back in Tucson, Terry was again immersed in watching his master weaver aunts, cousins, and other family members' lives revolve around Navajo weaving. With the passing of his mother, Rosann, in 1996, Terry found comfort in realizing that he could help out by fixing Navajo weaving tools and assisting his aunts with their prep work for their Navajo weaving classes. In the summer of 2009, Terry accompanied his daughter, Roxanne, to Idyllwild, where we were conducting Navajo weaving classes. With Roxanne enrolled in a summer art program, and at our invitation, he warped and wove his first Navajo rug in our class. Fellow students often interrupted him to ask him to fix their tools or adjust their looms, and he began thinking about various tools that he could make to speed up his work and solve issues for the students who had physical limitations. Up until then, his maternal uncle, Ernie Teller, and his uncle, Belvin Pete, were the designated toolmakers and loom builders for us. Both uncles happily gave him instructions, assistance, feedback, and encouragement to make looms and other Navajo weaving tools, and gifted him with some woodworking tools.

Terry has come full circle back to the days of growing up among his Navajo weaving family, and as he has acquired more woodworking tools, he has begun to shape battens and weaving combs and build more looms and other new tools.

Terry's daughter, Roxanne, is his biggest cheerleader and his biggest critic. As she is weaving, she might complain to Terry that her batten keeps snapping, or her fingers can't grasp the weft because the tension is too tight. With each request, Terry ponders the possibilities and then comes up with a tool. He created a batten with a more squared edge instead of the rounded traditional edge and it did not snap as much. He created a flat wood hook to smoothly glide through the warp strings to assist in grasping the weft when the warps are very tight. His crowning achievement came appropriately during the 2011 Thanksgiving holiday gathering of his family at his maternal grandmother's home, master weaver Ruth Teller. Terry showed a new comb that he had fashioned out of oak and called it a "Wolverine" because of how the teeth were slightly curved. His grandmother saw the comb and quickly announced that even though she can no longer weave, the comb was "a perfect comb" for weaving with an aging hand, the slight curve assisting in firmly packing in wool wefts. Earlier, Terry's grandmother had seen a selection

of his combs with burnt carvings and asked for a cute sheep to be drawn on her comb. She said, "I feel sad sometimes that I can no longer weave, but I can still hold a weaving comb and it helps me recall my happy memories of all my time spent weaving and how my weaving supported my family. I will hold this comb when my need to weave arises, which it does almost every day. I miss weaving." Now, Terry is constantly at his worktable, honing weaving tools for his family and for his growing base of customers. Whether Terry's Navajo weaving tools come adorned with decorative art or not, they all are functional for use in Navajo weaving. They are also "Navajo Grandmother Approved!"

COMBS ARE SPECIFIC TO A WEAVER'S NEEDS. THE SPACES NEED TO MATCH THE SPACING BETWEEN WARP THREADS. VARIATIONS CAN ACCOUNT FOR LEFT-HANDEDNESS, AND FOR AGE AND STRENGTH.

SIERRA NIZHONII TELLER ORNELAS

LOS ANGELES, CALIFORNIA

BORN OF THE WATER'S EDGE CLAN, *Tábąąhá*

BORN FOR THE MEXICAN PEOPLE CLAN, *Naakaii Dine'é*

MOTHER'S FATHER, WATER-FLOWS-TOGETHER CLAN,
Tó'aheedlíinii

FATHER'S FATHER, MEXICAN PEOPLE CLAN, *Naakaii Dine'é*

Barbara's daughter, Sierra, remembers learning the mechanics of weaving around the age of ten, but not really producing anything until she was sixteen. She modestly distinguishes between her talent and that of her brother, Michael, whom you will meet next: "I may weave, but my brother is a weaver." She wove mainly in a Two Grey Hills style when she started weaving, but quickly branched out into other traditional forms and period pieces, winning many awards with her work. But then she went beyond.

She wove a tapestry using an amusing *Pac-Man* motif from the popular computer game, and it was put on temporary exhibit at the Heard Museum, loom and all, unfinished. Then she wove two more tapestries, one female in one color and the other a male in a different color. Both characters had thought bubbles above them thinking of the other *Pac-Man*; it was titled *Forbidden Love*. She used it as her avatar on Facebook and it was noticed by the curators at the Hood Museum at Dartmouth College, whose curator came to Santa Fe Indian Market and bought the set. Her *Robot Man* is now in the permanent collection at the Wheelwright Museum in Santa Fe.

In 2004, Sierra graduated from the University of Arizona with a degree in media arts. Under the mentorship of textile scholar Dr. Ann Hedlund, she produced a weaving documentary titled *A Loom with a View*, a short film about contemporary Navajo weavers. Her mother, Barbara, her brother, Michael, and her great-aunt, Margaret Yazzie (see page 21), were featured. After graduation, she worked in Washington, D.C., at the Smithsonian's National Museum of the American Indian. In 2005, she took her first ribbon at the Santa Fe Indian Market, coming in third place in her weaving division. "The ribbon I won was for a Burntwater I wove in Washington, D.C. It was the first rug I wove living away from my parents. I felt immense freedom to find my voice, and it paid off."

"My brother and I get a lot of credit from our family for weaving styles that are considered 'nontraditional.' I know that my mother, Barbara, has come to admire the fact that my brother and I branched out with our weaving styles. Ironically, our inspiration for doing that came from her."

Sierra's brother, Michael, figured out that all eight-bit video games were basically pixelated images, made up of squares, so you could weave any image in an eight-bit game. Sierra asked Michael for permission to use his discovery, and this resulted in her award-winning *Pac-Man* suite. Later Barbara told Sierra and Michael she was concerned about what they were weaving, telling them that they should stick to more traditional styles. Sierra thought this was really funny, and told her mother the whole reason they were trying to be different was because that's how they saw her weave as children.

One family relic is a sampler rug (see page 19) that Sierra's grandmother, Nellie Peshlaki Teller, had woven to show to customers at the Two Grey Hills Trading Post; they would use it to pick out the style, color combination, and design elements they wanted in their rugs. It was a long, narrow rug, featuring more than ten styles: twills, geometrics, diagonals, and two-face styles. It was the first Teller "catalog." Barbara loved to show her children this sampler rug. Sierra thought it was an amazing mash-up of ideas. Respectfully, Sierra and

Michael explained to their mother that being different and trying new things was their family's tradition. Barbara was pretty amused by this. After that, she let them weave whatever they wanted as long as they wove a Two Grey Hills–style tapestry in between weaving other styles.

Sierra said, "I don't weave professionally, but I still have great respect for the art form of Navajo weaving. I'm currently a writer on a network sitcom, and I keep a loom in my office in Los Angeles. Whenever I'm blocked in my writing, or dealing with any kind of stress, I will turn to the loom, as my mom has always taught me to do. I will weave a few lines and try to find my balance again. There are a lot of similarities in my mother's profession as a weaver and mine as a writer. I truly feel like my mom and dad, through

A weaver's life is very up and down. Feast or famine. You have to work hard not only on your pieces, but also to be an advocate for your work, and an ambassador for your culture.

her work and his support of her career, have trained me for what I now do. A weaver's life is very up and down. Feast or famine. You have to work hard not only on your pieces, but also to be an advocate for your work, and an ambassador for your culture. Learning to weave gave me the grit and hustle I needed to succeed in writing. I also think writing influenced my weaving."

Sierra was one of two girls born in a generation of boys and felt a lot of pressure to weave at a very young age. Sierra says, "I can still remember sitting at the loom as a child and looming over me (no pun intended) were my mom, my aunts, and my grandma. I felt this intense pressure to carry on the tradition, to be as successful as my mom and her sisters and mother. I haven't been able to reach that success as a weaver, but it gives me such great pride to know that my brother, Michael, is well on his way to having a career as a master Navajo weaver. He'll definitely get there. Now I have a twenty-month-old son, Javier Teller Ornelas O'Mara, and I'm trying to get back into weaving so I'll have the skills to teach him. Who knows, maybe he'll come up with his own style, or he'll rebel and only weave Two Greys. As long as he's weaving."

MICHAEL PAUL TELLER ORNELAS

TUCSON, ARIZONA

BORN OF THE WATER'S EDGE CLAN, *Tábąąhá*

BORN FOR THE MEXICAN PEOPLE CLAN, *Naakaii Dine'é*

MOTHER'S FATHER, WATER-FLOWS-TOGETHER CLAN, *Tó'aheedlíinii*

FATHER'S FATHER, MEXICAN CLAN, *Naakaii Dine'é*

Michael has been weaving since he was thirteen, when he asked his mother to teach him. She set up a warp, and was amazed at how quickly he picked up the skills. At mere suggestions to watch his edges, weaving too tight, too loose, he was a quick study and started doing complex designs. When he was eighteen, his child's blanket earned Best of Show at the Heard Museum's 2003 student competition. Some of his tapestries are also in the Heard Museum's permanent collections.

As a computer science major at the University of Arizona, Michael used his computer to map out design ideas for his weavings early in his weaving career. During the same time, he took a part-time job with the Arizona State Museum's Gloria F. Ross Center for Tapestry Studies and worked as a web developer. He was tasked with creating a website that allowed users to search and explore the Joe Ben Wheat Southwest Textiles database. The Arizona State Museum had vast information on nineteenth-century Navajo blankets. The user could make search queries based on a rug's size, pattern, age,

MICHAEL'S COMPUTER SKILLS COME INTO PLAY IN HIS DESIGN WORK.

THIS SMALL TAPESTRY SHOWS A TREND AWAY FROM MINIATURES AND TOWARD A MORE TRADITIONAL SENSIBILITY. CONSTANT EXPLORATION OF POSSIBILITIES MARK MICHAEL'S WEAVING LIFE.

weaver, and handspun or commercially processed wool weft types. (The website, unfortunately, is no longer accessible.)

Michael says, "Weaving has always been about breaking barriers for me. I grew up with stories about how my mom challenged the status quo, selling directly to customers and museums instead of going through dealers and galleries. So I couldn't help but question why my mom, this trendsetter, was saying I couldn't branch out. Her standard response was, 'Because you just can't!'" Michael and his mother would laugh because they both knew it was not a good answer and after some talking, Barbara remembered having the same arguments with her mother. In time, his mother found trust in his ideas, letting go of her restrictions imposed by her mother and let Michael experiment with color and design.

Michael remarked, "Weaving designs have always been changing despite what we were initially taught. I looked for my surrounding environment like the weavers of old. They would use the surrounding environment of nature, of the land. I used my current surroundings of technology and electronics. So while weaving designs have always been changing, the challenges and skills of weaving will always connect us together."

Some years, the economy has resulted in a down market for Indian art collectibles, so Michael started weaving miniatures with design motifs from pop culture, video game avatars, and Japanese anime, as well as traditional Navajo design elements, and he put these textiles into art frames. Younger people started their weaving collections with his miniatures, and they would not just buy one; most bought two to four at each show.

Michael says, "I've been doing tapestry miniatures for a long time. Small weavings that are around five inches by five inches because they let me quickly prototype and experiment with design elements—abstracts or my family's traditional Navajo designs. It's been a ton of fun to see what I can do with designs and colors." Recently he's been moving back into weaving larger pieces, though. "I want to take what I learned doing the miniatures and apply it to large-scale projects. I've been working with my mother on a few projects. We will usually call each other into our workrooms to trade ideas and conference about patterns and problems. It has been a validating experience to have my mom, the great master weaver, reliably come to me when she's having an issue. And, of course, she's been a great resource for me with her years of experience and knowledge."

Michael had four of his tapestries, a Two Grey Hills tapestry, a pop culture–influenced pictorial on the comic book hero, *Spider-Man*, and two of his signature miniature weavings—a complete representation of his weaving styles—on exhibit at the Amerind Foundation and Museum in Dragoon, Arizona. The exhibit featured contemporary weavings by young Diné artists entitled *Gifts from Spider Woman's Grandchildren* in 2012.

Today, Michael has moved away a bit from being inspired by pop culture for his rug designs. He explains, "It's not that I'm not influenced by it, but my focus is more on the complexity of my designs. How far is too much? How strong is simple? How do I keep a good rhythm and balance between all the elements of the rug? I'm confident that I am better than I was five years ago, but I still wish to be better than I am today." During the 2017 Santa Fe Indian Market in Santa Fe, New Mexico, Michael's Two Grey Hills tapestry was purchased by the Museum of Indian Arts and Culture and will be exhibited along with Barbara's and my Two Grey Hills tapestries and a Burntwater tapestry by granddaughter Roxanne. Michael is doing the full circle back to his traditional roots of weaving mainly Two Grey Hills tapestries and Barbara and I, we are smiling from ear to ear!

HERE ARE TWO OF MICHAEL'S FRAMED MINIATURES— ABSTRACTS THAT WALK THE LINE BETWEEN CONTEMPORARY AND TRADITIONAL SYMBOLOGY.

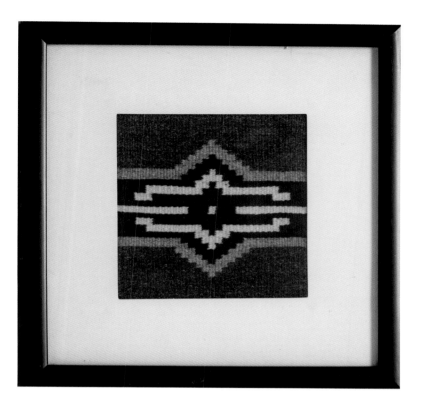

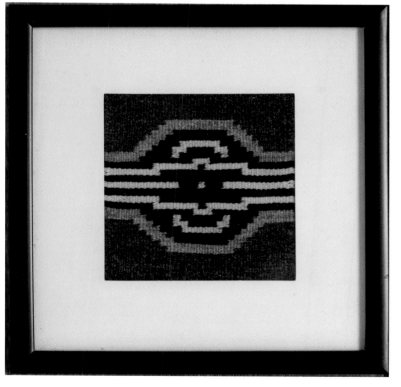

ROXANNE ROSE LEE

TUCSON, ARIZONA

BORN OF THE MEXICAN PEOPLE CLAN, *Naakaii Dine'é*

BORN FOR THE WATER'S EDGE CLAN, *Tábąąhá*

FATHER'S FATHER, RED BOTTOM PEOPLE, *Tł'ááshchí'í*

Roxanne Rose Lee is a seventh-generation Navajo weaver, sixteen years old, and in the eleventh grade. She is the granddaughter of master weaver Rosann Teller Lee, and is grandniece to Barbara Teller Ornelas and me, Lynda Teller Pete—though according to Navajo custom, we call her our granddaughter, too. Roxanne's mother, Julie Charles, is in the U.S. Army and stationed at Fort Lewis, Washington, currently serving her seventeenth year. Roxanne lives in Tucson with her father, Terry Lee, Navajo weaving tool craftsmen and a self-employed artist.

Barbara and I began to teach Roxanne how to weave very early—at age four! When young children are first introduced to a Navajo loom during Barbara's and my Navajo weaving classes, most grab the warps and pull and bang on things with the weaving tools, seeing the loom and tools as new toys. But when my husband, Belvin, sat Roxanne in front of a Navajo loom for the first time, she strummed her fingers across the warps, picked up each color of the wool and tucked them inside the male/female warps, and flipped the batten up as an experienced weaver would do. We looked at each other in astonishment that Roxanne innately knew how to treat the Navajo loom at age four.

AS A SEVENTH-GENERATION WEAVER, ROXANNE TAKES HER RESPONSIBILITY TO HER HERITAGE AND HER FAMILY SERIOUSLY.

Roxanne says, "Navajo weaving is a way of life for my dad's side of the family. I got my first loom when I was four, and finished my first rug, a colorful sampler woven with commercial wool, when I was ten. My grandma Lynda bought it."

When Roxanne finishes her homework on school days, she weaves two hours a day, and more hours on the weekend. She received her first blue ribbon in 2013 at the Santa Fe Indian Market for a small rug woven with her own design elements using commercial wool. This rug was sold along with her grandmother Barbara's rug, and she is happy both weavings will be together.

Roxanne said, "Weaving is very important in our family. For four summers, I have spent two weeks in my grandmothers' annual Navajo weaving class at Idyllwild School of Arts. In each of those summers, I have finished one or two weavings and have entered them in the youth division at Santa Fe Indian Market." These rugs Roxanne finished in our classes were woven with commercial wool and, important to note, she wove her own designs in them—unlike us when we were her age. Roxanne says her rugs have no particular Navajo style, just her own style. Each rug entered into the Santa Fe Indian Market has received ribbons, all first places, and all have sold.

Roxanne says, "My grandmothers have told me about our Navajo history and our relatives' weaving history, but it wasn't until I was in the classroom and watching other kids my age learning for the first time that I realized how important it was for me to know my history. I think it is important to know your history, and if some kids my age do not know how to weave, there should be places for them to learn. My grandmothers told me about Navajo organizations that seek funding to help Navajo kids and maybe adults to learn how to weave or to receive assistance in selling their work. I think this is a good idea and if I can help when I become more experienced, I would like to do that."

In 2017, Roxanne entered her Burntwater-style tapestry, her first tapestry using very fine weft wool spun by her grandmother Barbara's and my vegetal dyed wool, in the Navajo Weaving Youth Division at the Santa Fe Indian Market, and won first place. Her tapestry was bought by the Museum of Indian Arts and Culture in Santa Fe, New Mexico, and will be exhibited along with the tapestries of Barbara, Lynda, and her uncle Michael.

I think it is important to know your history, and if some kids my age do not know how to weave, there should be places for them to learn.

Roxanne's quest for weaving inspiration is amazing; her zeal for creation is fearless beyond artistic boundaries. In all the years that I have taught people, all ages, both genders, diverse nationalities, there are standouts every now and then, and I feel proud to be a part of their weaving journeys. Much to my delight, here in my own family, Roxanne is a standout as a young Navajo weaving artist with a strong desire to maintain her own Navajo traditions.

ROXANNE'S GREAT-AUNT LYNDA TAKES HER RESPONSIBILITY AS A MENTOR SERIOUSLY AS WELL.

A GALLERY OF RUG STYLES MENTIONED IN THIS BOOK

Definitive descriptions of rug styles are fraught with exceptions because rug styles are not static. They evolve over time, distance, and historical events. Weavers move from one area to another through marriage or circumstance; they are influenced by teachers of different backgrounds and experiences. They create from different materials and dyestuffs, and may use commercially prepared fiber and yarn. They apply their own aesthetic and life experience to their work. The examples given here are meant to suggest some of the styles that one might encounter, not to define precise categories.

We are grateful to Jackson Clark and Toh-Atin Gallery of Durango, Colorado, for providing the rug style photographs. Except where noted, all photographs by McKayla Lee.

CRYSTAL. Dating back to the 1920s, early Crystal rugs were influenced by trader J. B. Moore. They have bold motifs and strong geometric borders with hooks, frets, and other lively elements. Contemporary Crystal rugs, like the one below, use more vegetal dyes and might have no borders.

WEAVER UNKNOWN.

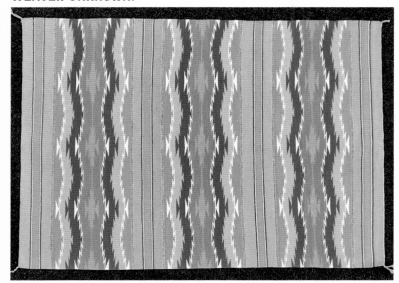

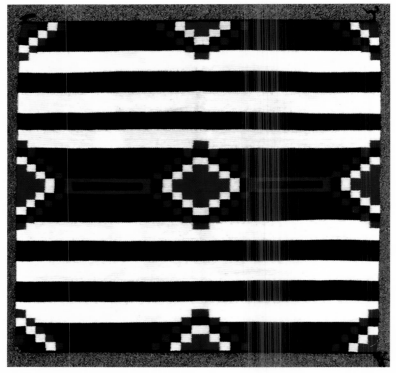

WOVEN BY NELLIE SHORTY BEGAY.

CHIEF BLANKETS:
FIRST, SECOND, AND THIRD PHASE.

First Phase blankets dating from the 18th century to about 1840 are generally composed of simple, narrow horizontal stripes in natural wool colors, perhaps with indigo or red accents derived from raveled yarn.

Second Phase blankets were woven up until about 1860. Their horizontal bands might be accented with small rectangles or diamonds.

Third Phase blankets date from about 1860 until 1868, the end of the Long Walk. These blankets have bold diamond and rectangular motifs at the top, middle, and bottom.

Today we see revival versions of the chief blankets, especially Third Phase, as in the rug shown above.

CHINLE. This style was influenced by Mary Cabot Wheelwright and trader Cozy McSparron. It is often characterized by natural dyes in warm, muted earth hues of greens, golds, tans, and pinks, or by natural wool colors as in the rug below. Horizontal stripes of repeating geometric patterns alternate with plain bands, and usually no borders are present.

WOVEN BY BERTHA HARVEY.

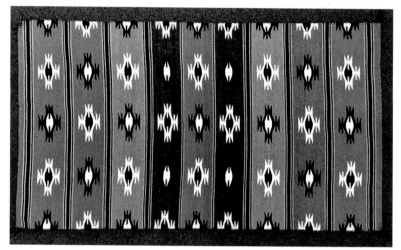

BURNTWATER. This style from the Toadlena/Crystal area dates from the 1960s. Patterning is similar to Two Grey Hills but uses pastel hues derived from vegetal dyes. It is characterized by complex geometric borders and end panels.

WEAVER UNKNOWN.

WEAVER UNKNOWN.

EYE DAZZLER. As the name implies, this style includes bright colors and serrated patterns, often bold zigzags and diamonds outlined in a single contrasting color to create a striking optical effect.

GANADO. The Hubbell Trading Post near Ganado, Arizona, originated this style. Many are called "Ganado Reds" because of the deep red motifs offset by gray, black, and white. These rugs are bordered with large geometric motifs.

WOVEN BY CLARA YAZZIE.

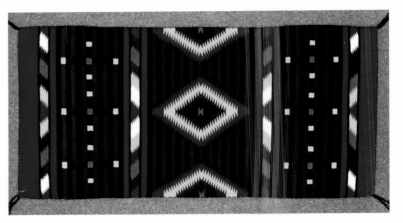

WOVEN BY MILLICENT PLATERO.

GERMANTOWN REVIVAL. Bruce Burnham, owner of Burnham Trading Company in Sanders, Arizona, encouraged this style. Featuring bands of repeating geometric motifs and plain or striped bands of contrasting colors, these rugs are inspired by the original Germantown style, which developed in the mid-nineteenth century. Germantown refers to the area in Pennsylvania that produced the commercial yarns commonly used in Navajo rugs during this period.

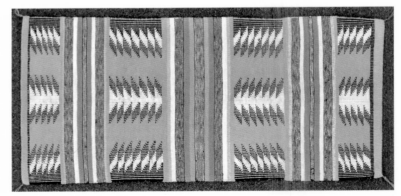

WOVEN BY SUSIE BEGAY.

RAISED OUTLINE. Created by Coal Mine Mesa weavers in the 1960s, these rugs are characterized by an exacting technique in which the weaver uses weft threads comprised of two contrasting colors, twisting the two on each other to create raised ridges or ribs. This raised texture is visible on only one side.

MOKI, OR MOQUI. These rugs usually have narrow horizontal background stripes, often alternating dark blue or black with dark gray or brown. Large geometric motifs overlay the background.

WOVEN BY FRANCES DRAKE.

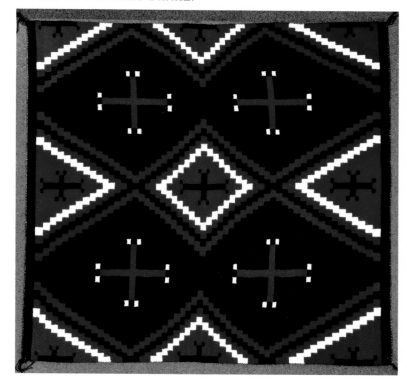

WOVEN BY BARBARA TELLER ORNELAS FROM HANDSPUN YARN. IN THE PERMANENT COLLECTION OF THE HEARD MUSEUM, PHOENIX, ARIZONA.

TWO GREY HILLS. Originating in the Chuska Mountains in the 1920s and promoted by the Two Grey Hills Trading Post, these classic rugs are bordered with four matching corner elements and a large center diamond or multiple diamonds. They are known for using blended natural colors of wool and having high weft counts.

TEEC NOS POS. Generally large, bold, and colorful, these rugs have elaborate geometric or zigzag borders. They are reminiscent of classic Oriental rugs.

WOVEN BY BESSIE BLACKGOAT.

TWILL. This is a thick, reversible weave structure that is often used in saddle blankets, which are tightly woven in either single or double sizes.

WEAVER UNKNOWN.

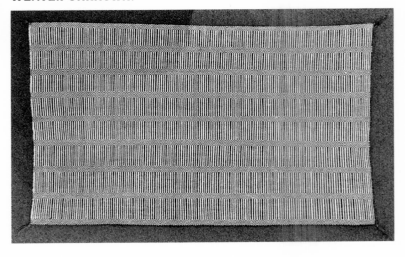

STORM PATTERN.

WOVEN BY LYNDA TELLER PETE. THE FOUR SACRED MOUNTAINS AT THE CORNERS LEAD INTO THE CENTER, THE CENTER OF THE UNIVERSE OR THE HOGAN OR HOMEPLACE. ABOVE AND BELOW THE HOMEPLACE ARE ELECTRICAL CHARGES; LIGHTNING RODS ARE ON EITHER SIDE. AT THE TOP AND BOTTOM ARE WATER BEETLES—GUARDIANS OF THE UNIVERSE. PHOTOGRAPH BY LYNDA TELLER PETE.

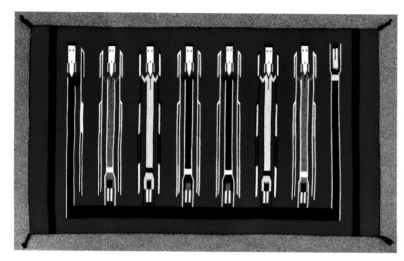

WOVEN BY M. HARRISON.

YEI. These incorporate stylized representations of sacred Yei Bi Chei dancers. Male Yei have round heads, and females have square heads.

VEGETAL DYED AND WOVEN BY EVELYN MARTIN.

WIDE RUINS. This style was influenced by Sallie Wagner and Bill Lippincott, owners of the Wide Ruins Trading Post in Arizona. They are characterized by soft pastels of natural dyed yarns.

WOVEN BY LENA BEGAY.

TREE OF LIFE. Dating back to the late 1800s, these pictorial rugs originated in the northern part of the Navajo Nation. A cornstalk, birds, flowers, and rainbow bands are common.

TRADITIONAL NAVAJO LOOM

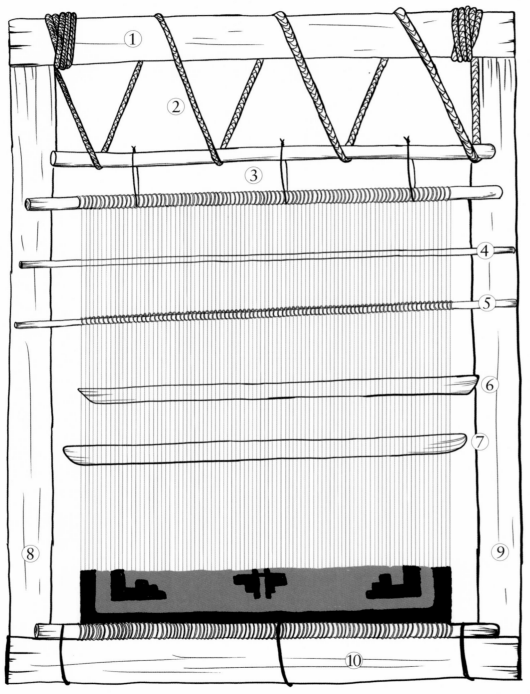

LOOM KEY

1 Sky Beam (top beam)
2 Male and Female Lightning (tension cord)
3 The Clouds (space between the tension bar and the loom bar)
4 Male Rain (shed rod)
5 Female Rain (heddle rod)
6 Sunrays (batten for male warp)
7 Rainbow (batten for female warp)
8 Female Gravity (left vertical post)
9 Male Gravity (right vertical post)
10 Earth Beam (bottom beam)

Illustration by Mychal Yellowman
Labels by Lyle Harvey

RESOURCES

PUBLICATIONS

Allen, Carter. *The Weavers Way: Navajo Profiles.* Carter Allen, 2003.

Benally, Malcolm D., ed., foreword by Jennifer Nez Denetdale. *Bitter Water: Diné Oral Histories of the Navajo-Hopi Land Dispute.* Tucson: University of Arizona Press, 2011.

Brugge, David M. *The Navajo-Hopi Land Dispute: An American Tragedy.* Albuquerque: University of New Mexico Press, 1994.

Denetdale, Jennifer. *The Long Walk: The Forced Navajo Exile.* Langhorne, Pennsylvania: Chelsea House, 2007.

Denetdale, Jennifer Nez. *Reclaiming Diné History: The Legacies of Navajo Chief Manuelito and Juanita.* Tucson: University of Arizona Press, 2007.

Hedlund, Ann Lane. *Navajo Weaving in the Late Twentieth Century: Kin, Community, and Collectors.* Tucson: University of Arizona Press, 2004.

Hedlund, Ann Lane. *Navajo Weaving: The Santa Fe Collection.* Oklahoma City, Oklahoma: National Cowboy Hall of Fame, 1997.

Hedlund, Ann Lane. *Reflections of the Weaver's World: The Gloria F. Ross Collection of Contemporary Navajo Weaving.* Denver, Colorado: Denver Art Museum, 1992.

Iverson, Peter, and Monty Roessel. *Diné: A History of the Navajos.* Albuquerque: University of New Mexico Press, 2015.

James, H. L. *Rugs and Posts: The Story of Navajo Weaving and Indian Trading.* Atglen, Pennsylvania: Schiffer, 1999.

Johnson, Broderick, and Ruth Roessel. *Navajo Livestock Reduction: A National Disgrace.* Tsaile, Arizona: Navajo Community College Press, 1974.

Kammer, Jerry. *The Second Long Walk: The Navajo-Hopi Land Dispute.* Albuquerque: University of New Mexico Press, 1987.

Lee, Lloyd L., ed., foreword by Gregory Cajete. *Diné Perspectives: Revitalizing and Reclaiming Navajo Thought.* Tucson: University of Arizona Press, 2014.

M'Closkey, Kathy. *Swept Under the Rug: A Hidden History of Navajo Weaving.* Albuquerque: University of New Mexico Press, 2008.

McManis, Kent, and Robert Jeffries. *Navajo Weavings.* Tucson: Rio Nuevo, 2009.

Webster, Laurie D., Louise Stiver, D. Y. Begay, and Lynda Teller Pete. *Navajo Textiles: The Crane Collection at the Denver Museum of Nature and Science.* Denver, Colorado: Denver Museum of Nature and Science, 2017.

Weisiger, Marsha, and William Cronon. *Dreaming of Sheep in Navajo Country.* Seattle: University of Washington Press, 2011.

Wheat, Joe Ben. *Blanket Weaving in the Southwest,* edited by Ann Lane Hedlund. Tucson: University of Arizona Press, 2003.

Wilkins, Teresa J. *Patterns of Exchange: Navajo Weavers and Traders*. Norman, Oklahoma: University of Oklahoma Press, 2008.

Yazzie, Ethelou. *Navajo History*. Tsaile, Arizona: Navajo Community College Press, 1971.

Salena Bookshelf, Inc. (www.salenabookshelf.com) has a selection of Navajo language and other Navajo-related books.

VIDEO LINKS

A Loom with a View: https://youtu.be/HkAggO4D8Og
A 13-minute video produced for the Arizona State Museum by Sierra Teller Ornelas and Justin Thomas, featuring three generations of the Teller family: Margaret Yazzie, Barbara Teller Ornelas, and Michael Teller Ornelas.

Master Artist Workshop: Navajo Weaving: https://youtu.be/ZlgY3p2kXVw
An 8-minute video produced by the Heard Museum, featuring the authors teaching a three-day workshop to Navajo students.

Craft in America: https://youtu.be/axGeXfOPU84
A segment of the Craft in America series produced by PBS, featuring Barbara Teller Ornelas and Lynda Teller Pete teaching Navajo weaving in Canyon de Chelly.

OTHER RESOURCES

Amerind Foundation and Museum: Collections, library, educational outreach, research, and exhibitions. 2100 N. Amerind Rd., Dragoon, AZ 85609. www.amerind.org.

Brown Sheep Company: Family-owned yarn mill producing wool, fine wool, and yarn. 100662 Co Rd 16, Mitchell, NE 69357. www.brownsheep.com.

Crownpoint Rug Auction: Monthly auction of Navajo rugs. Main St H-1, Crownpoint, NM 87313. www.crownpointrugauction.com.

Denver Museum of Science and Nature: Collections, conservation, research, and exhibitions. 2001 Colorado Blvd, Denver, CO 80205. www.dmns.org.

Gloria F. Ross Center for Tapestry Studies: Research projects and public programs exploring traditional and contemporary handwoven tapestry worldwide. Arizona State Museum, University of Arizona Campus, Tucson, AZ. www.tapestrycenter.org.

Hubbell Trading Post Historic Site: Historic homestead, trading post, interpretive exhibitions, workshops, and auctions. Hwy. 191, Ganado, AZ 86505. www.nps.gov/hutr/index.htm.

Heard Museum: Dedicated to the advancement of Native American arts, the museum has world-class collections, exhibitions,and archives. The Heard Museum Guild sponsors the annual Indian Fair and Market each spring. www.heard.org.

Idyllwild Arts Academy: Summer sessions in Navajo weaving and more. 52500 Temecula Road, Idyllwild, CA 92549. www.idyllwildarts.org.

Museum of Indian Arts and Culture/Laboratory of Anthropology: Collections, programs, and research. 710 Camino Lejo, Santa Fe, NM 87505. www.miaclab.org.

Navajo Nation Museum: Library, collections, exhibits, and programming focusing on cultural history of the Navajo. Highway 264 and Post Office Loop, Window Rock, AZ 86515. www.navajonationmuseum.org.

Navajo Sheep Project: Dedicated to preserving and breeding back the Navajo-Churro sheep. PO Box 6445, North Logan, UT 84322. www.navajosheepproject.com.

Santa Fe Indian Market: Sponsored by Southwestern Association for Indian Arts the third weekend in August each year. www.swaia.org.

Sheep is Life, Dibé be' liná: An organization that promotes sustainable livelihood and traditional Navajo values. It hosts a festival every June. www.navajolifeway.org.

Smithsonian's National Museum of the American Indian: Committed to advancing knowledge and understanding of the Native cultures of the Western Hemisphere through research, educational outreach, and exhibitions. 4th St SW & Independence Ave SW, Washington, DC 20560. www. nmai.si.edu.

Toh-Atin Gallery: Nationally recognized gallery for Native American art. 145 W 9th St, Durango, CO 81301. www. toh-atin.com.

Wheelwright Museum of the American Indian: Unique exhibitions of contemporary and historic Native American art. 704 Camino Lejo, Santa Fe, NM 87505. www.wheelwright.org.

INDEX

MORE BOOKS FROM THRUMS YOU MIGHT ENJOY

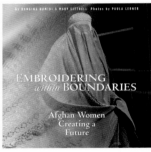

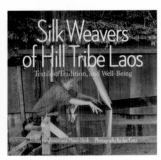

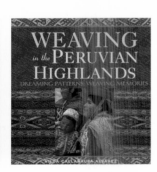

ThrumsBooks.com